A1

Extra Language Trainer

John Stevens · Marion Karg · Frauke Mönkeberg

Beratende Mitarbeit

Christine House, Berlin
Frauke Mönkeberg, Bielefeld
Silvia Nienhaus, Bergisch-Gladbach
Dietlind Unger, Leipzig

Englisch für Erwachsene

First Choice

Cornelsen

Welcome!

In dieser kurzen Einleitung erfahren Sie das Wichtigste über den *First Choice A1 Extra Language Trainer* und wie Sie mit ihm am effektivsten arbeiten können.

Zielsetzung

Wie der Name schon sagt, bietet der *Extra Language Trainer* zusätzliche Übungsmöglichkeiten zu Ihrem Kursbuch *First Choice A1* oder *First Choice A1 Fast*. Den *Extra Language Trainer* können Sie zu unterschiedlichen Zwecken einsetzen:

- zur allgemeinen Wiederholung und Festigung des Lernstoffs aus dem Kursbuch;
- zur Aufarbeitung von Lerninhalten, bei denen Sie das Gefühl haben, dass Sie diese noch nicht richtig beherrschen;
- als Stütze und Ergänzung, wenn Sie verpasste Unterrichtsstunden in Eigenarbeit nachholen;
- zur Erweiterung Ihres Sprachkönnens, indem Sie das Gelernte in neuen, teilweise weitergehenden Zusammenhängen anwenden.

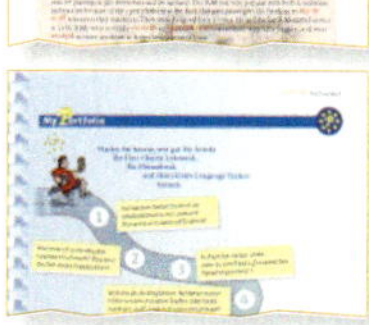

Aufbau und Inhalt

Der *Extra Language Trainer* umfasst zwölf Units, die denen Ihres Kursbuchs entsprechen. Die Units sind jeweils in überschaubare Abschnitte gegliedert:

Vocabulary & Phrases
Übungen zu Wortschatz und Redewendungen;

Grammar
Übungen und Übersichten zur Grammatik;

Mixed Bag
Übungen zu verschiedenen Lernbereichen einschließlich einer Erweiterungsübung ***English for eXperts***, wie Sie sie aus dem *Magazine* des Kursbuchs kennen;

The Real Thing
Lesetexte und authentische Materialien aus dem wirklichen Leben;

My Portfolio
Lerntechniken, Kontrolle und Selbsteinschätzung Ihres Lernerfolgs sowie das Sammeln von eigenen Texten und Materialien in Ihrem ganz persönlichen „Dossier".

Die ersten Units enthalten nicht alle Abschnitte, wobei Sie hier noch einige extra Lerntipps erhalten.

Innerhalb der Units finden Sie kurze Zusammenfassungen und Beispiele der zentralen grammatischen Aspekte der jeweiligen Unit (***Remember***). Die kleinen gelben ***Notes*** weisen auf bestimmte Fallstricke und typische Fehlerquellen hin, auf die Sie achten sollten.

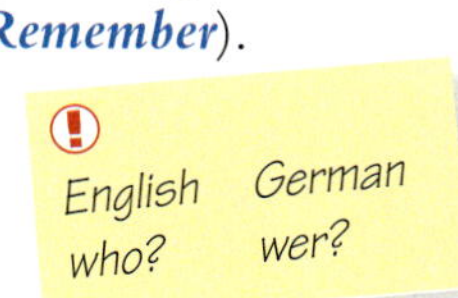

Wie arbeite ich mit dem *Extra Language Trainer*?

Das Übungsmaterial im *Extra Language Trainer* ist zur Nacharbeit gedacht, d.h. parallel zu den Units im Kursbuch oder auch am Ende einer Unit. Am besten in regelmäßigen Abständen. Haben Sie jedoch das Gefühl, dass Sie mit einer Kursbuchlektion gut zurechtkommen, so können Sie auch vorher mit den Übungen des *Extra Language Trainer* beginnen.

Sie können die Übungen und Abschnitte grundsätzlich in beliebiger Reihenfolge bearbeiten; es ist jedoch zu beachten, dass in *Vocabulary & Phrases*, *Grammar* und *Mixed Bag* einfachere Übungen jeweils am Anfang stehen. Wollen Sie also vom Leichten zum Schwierigeren vorgehen, halten Sie sich besser an die vorgegebene Reihenfolge. Der Abschnitt *The Real Thing* ist meist anspruchsvoller und bietet sich deshalb gut als Abschluss an: der Wortschatz, den Sie hier finden, geht in jedem Fall über den des Kursbuchkapitels hinaus. Jede Unit schließt mit *My Portfolio* ab: Sie lernen Tipps, Tricks, Arbeitstechniken und Methoden für das Sprachenlernen kennen, Ihre eigenen Lernfortschritte („das-kann-ich-bereits") einzuschätzen, Ihre Sprachlernaktivitäten zu überprüfen und Sie legen separat in einem Ordner Ihr eigenes „Dossier" an, wobei Sie hier eigene Arbeiten aller Art, die Sie für gelungen halten, aufbewahren.

Lösungsschlüssel

Sämtliche Lösungen finden Sie im ***Key*** ab Seite 82. Gehen Sie jedoch so vor, dass Sie Ihre Antworten erst nach der Bearbeitung überprüfen, wenn Sie die Aufgaben und Lösungen noch einmal durchgesehen haben. Wenn Sie dann beim Abgleich mit dem ***Key*** feststellen, dass bestimmte Übungsteile nicht richtig beantwortet wurden, schauen Sie im Kursbuch und Ihren Unterrichtsmitschriften nach Hilfe und wiederholen Sie die Übung zu einem späteren Zeitpunkt. Im ***Vocabulary A–Z*** ab Seite 94 finden Sie die Vokabeln zum Nachschlagen. Sollten dann noch Fragen offen bleiben, fragen Sie in Ihrem Kurs und bei Ihrer Kursleitung nach.

Grundsätzlich gilt, wie bei allem Lernen, dass Sie effektiver und mit besserem Erfolg üben und lernen, wenn Sie mehrere kürzere Übungsblöcke einplanen und nicht versuchen, eine ganze Unit auf einmal „durchzuackern".

First Choice im Internet

Besuchen Sie *First Choice* im Internet!
Auf der *First Choice* Webseite **www.cornelsen-firstchoice.de** finden Sie weitere Materialien zum Weiterlernen sowie das *Journal* mit aktuellen landeskundlichen Informationen.

Und nun viel Erfolg und viel Spaß wünschen Ihnen

Autorenteam und Redaktion

Table of contents

First contact

1 Bilden Sie Gruppen von jeweils drei Wörtern, die zusammengehören.

Family

partner

______

______

Jobs

______

______

______

Transport

______

______

______

Food

______

______

______

bus • computer programmer • father • journalist • mother • ~~partner~~ • pizza
plane • sandwich • spaghetti • taxi • teacher

2 Ordnen Sie die Wörter neu, sodass sich sinnvolle Ausdrücke ergeben.

~~have the wrong~~	name	have the wrong number
make a phone	journalist	
a flight	expert	
my first	teacher	
an English	ticket	
a computer	call	
a travel	~~number~~	

3 Ergänzen Sie.

at

on

to

1 Welcome *to* Germany!

2 Sorry, Sarah is away ______ business.

3 Look ______ this, Dave.

4 Say hello ______ Nina for me, please.

4 Ergänzen Sie die Sprechblasen mit einer passenden Frage oder Äußerung.

are • English • for • from? • ~~Gerlinde.~~ • ~~I'm~~ • meet • Nice • No • Oh, • problem.
sorry. • the • to • 'Ungarn'? • What's • Where • you • you.

1 *I'm Gerlinde.* Nice to meet you, Gerlinde.

2 You must have the wrong number. ____________

3 I'm sorry I'm late. ____________

4 ____________ Me? I'm from Berlin. And you?

5 My name's Nora, and this is Jason. ____________

6 ____________ The English for 'Ungarn'? It's 'Hungary'.

5 Folgende Sätze würde man im Englischen so nicht sagen. Korrigieren Sie die Sätze entsprechend.

1 Ben ~~is journalist~~.	Ben *is a journalist.*
2 Hello, darling. ~~I am it~~.	Hello, darling. ____________ .
3 I'm from Germany. ~~I am born~~ in Berlin.	I'm from Germany. ____________ in Berlin.
4 I'm sorry, ~~I'm too late~~.	I'm sorry, ____________ .

6 "False friends"

English for eXperts

In dieser Unit haben Sie gesehen, dass Sie viele englische Wörter bereits kennen. Bei einer Reihe von Wörtern, die wir auch im Deutschen gebrauchen, ist jedoch Vorsicht geboten! Diese *false friends* haben im Englischen eine andere Bedeutung und können daher von Muttersprachlern missverstanden werden. Ordnen Sie die Wörter in der linken Spalte ihren wirklichen Entsprechungen zu.

Oldtimer ☐	☐ city centre
Handy ☐	☐ dinner jacket,
City ☐	☐ mobile phone
Smoking ☐	☐ potato crisps
Beamer ☐	☐ veteran car
Kartoffelchips ☐	☐ bench
Pommes Frites ☐	☐ chips
(Park-)Bank ☐	☐ (video) projector

! Chips = Pommes Frites

The *Real* Thing

1 **Welche dieser Zeichen drücken Gegensätze aus?**

3

1

2

6

4

5

7

8

1 + ______ ______ + ______ ______ + ______

2 **Welche Schilder konnten Sie nicht mit einem anderen in Verbindung bringen? Können Sie die Bedeutung erahnen?**

My Portfolio

Finden Sie heraus, wie gut Sie bereits Ihr *First Choice Lehrwerk*, Ihr *Phrasebook* und Ihren *Extra Language Trainer* kennen.

1. Auf welchen Seiten finde ich die Inhaltsübersicht im Kursbuch? Wie nennt sich diese auf Englisch?
2. Was finde ich am Ende jedes Kapitels im Lehrwerk? Was sind die Ziele dieser Doppelseiten?
3. Auf welchen Seiten steht mehr zu dem Thema „Europäisches Sprachenportfolio"?
4. Wo habe ich die Möglichkeit, die Namen meiner Mitlernenden und deren Telefon- oder Mobilnummern und E-Mail-Adressen einzutragen?
5. Auf welcher/n Seite(n) werden die grammatischen Begriffe noch einmal kurz erklärt, z. B. was ein Adjektiv oder ein Gerundium ist. Wie werden diese auf Englisch bezeichnet?
6. Zu welchen Teilen im Kursbuch finde ich Lösungen? Wo?
7. Wo finde ich die Lösungen zu den Aufgaben des *Extra Language Trainer*?
8. Wo kann ich im *Phrasebook* Orte, Namen und Nationalitäten nachschlagen?
9. Die Hörtexte aus den Bereichen der Unit, *Magazine* und *Quick Check* lassen sich nachlesen. Wo?
10. Warum befindet sich beim Bookmark am oberen Rand eine Aussparung? *Tipp:* Legen Sie das Bookmark auf eine Seite im *Phrasebook*.
11. Im alphabetischen Wörterverzeichnis des *Phrasebook* findet sich bei dem Eintrag ‚cellphone' die Abkürzung „AE". Was bedeutet diese?

2 Name, phone & email

1 Was ist das? Ergänzen Sie.

1 a h o t e l r o o m

2 a _ _ _ _ _ _ _ _ _ _ _

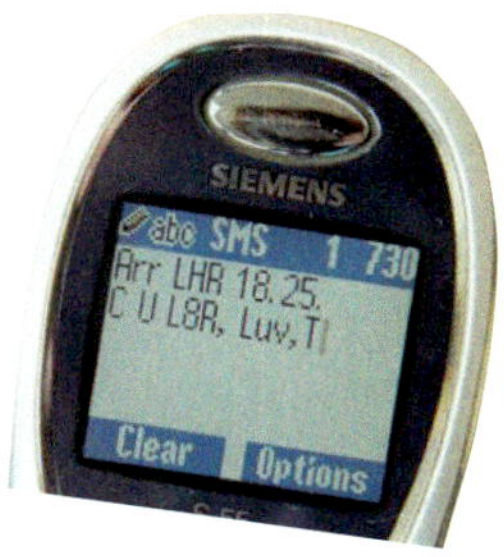

3 a _ _ _ _ _ _ _ _ _ _ _

4 a _ _ _ _ _ _ _ _ _ _ _

5 an _ _ _ _ _ _ _ _ _ _ _ _

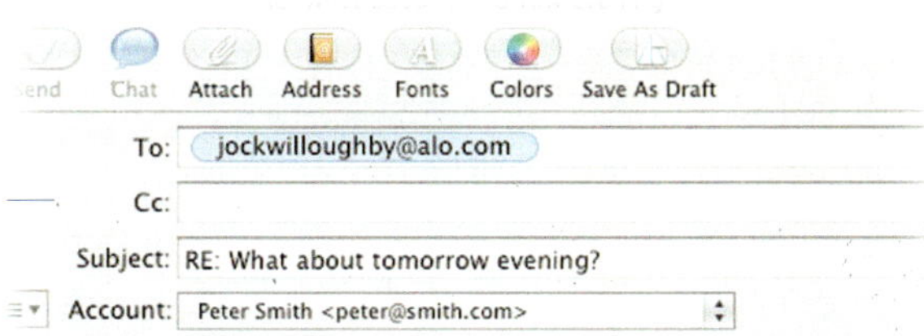

Nun ergänzen Sie die Sätze mit den Begriffen aus 1-5.

6 I have a very nice *hotel room*. It's a big double room.

7 Sorry, I don't have an ______ ______. I don't have internet.

8 When you arrive, send me a ______ ______, please.

9 Your ______ ______ – is it Mastercard or Visa?

10 My ______ ______ is 030 for Berlin, then 89584-8410.

2 Bilden Sie Wortpaare. Ein Begriff ist jeweils im anderen enthalten.

book • day • ~~photo~~ • hotel • letter • page • ~~passport~~ • room • evening • word

photo and *passport*

________ and ________

________ and ________

________ and ________

________ and ________

Ergänzen Sie nun die Begriffe von oben.

1 I think the *photo* in my *passport* is nice!

2 The first ________ of the ________ 'repeat' is 'r'.

3 I'm in a nice single ________ in the Queen's ________.

4 Look at ________ 10 in your ________, please.

5 The meeting is at the end of the ________, in the ________.

3 Bringen Sie die Sprechblasen in die richtige Reihenfolge, sodass sich ein Gespräch daraus ergibt.

___ Gaunt.

___ Sorry, what was that again?

___ Harry.

___ And what's your phone number, please?

___ Ah, Gaunt. And what's your first name, Mr Gaunt?

2 Yes, it's Gaunt.

! 020 = "oh two oh"
7273621 = "seven two seven, three six two one"

___ 020-7273621.

5 Oh, can you spell that for me, please?

1 Can I have your name, please?

___ Sorry, I don't have a mobile.

___ G-A-U-N-T.

___ 020-7273621, OK I've got that. And your mobile number?

4 **Ergänzen Sie die Schecks, indem Sie die Beträge in Worten ausschreiben.**

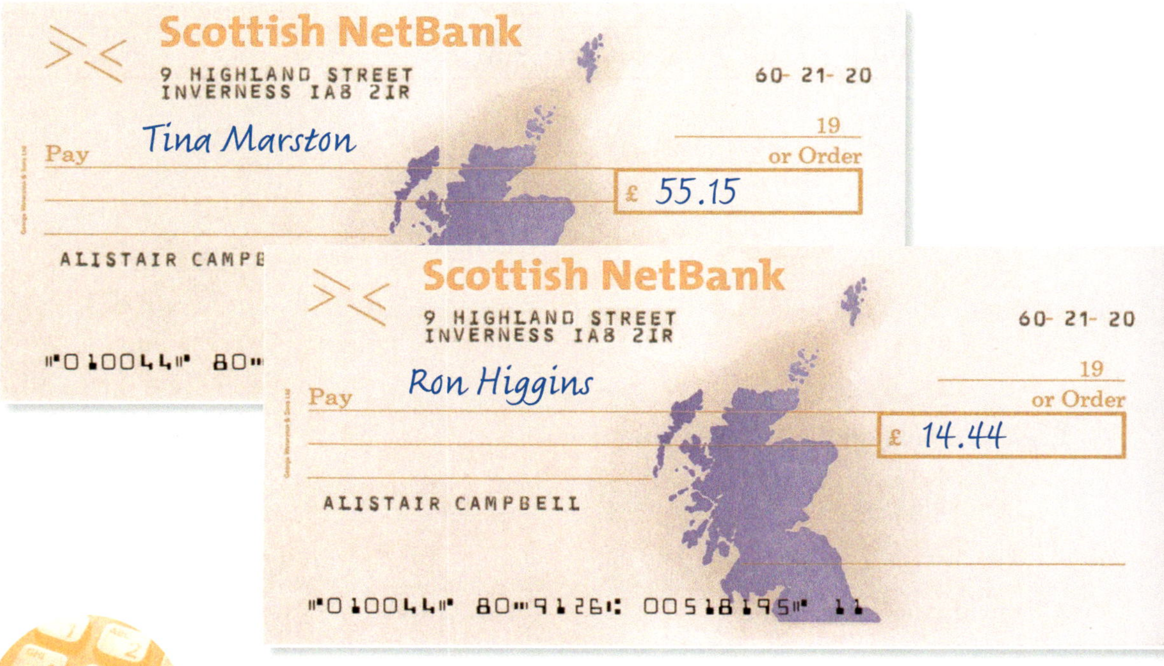

5 **0602 – 915477** **Finden Sie diese Telefonnummer in der Liste.**

- ☐ oh six oh two, nine one six seven three
- ☐ oh six oh three, one nine five four double seven
- ☐ oh six oh two, nine one five four two seven
- ☐ oh six oh two, nine one five four double seven
- ☐ oh two oh six, nine two five four eight seven

Remember **Zahlen**

-teen	six**teen**, seven**teen**, …	Schreibweise beachten: th**ir**teen, fi**f**teen, eigh**t**een, …
-ty	six**ty**, seven**ty**, …	Schreibweise beachten: fo**r**ty, fi**f**ty, eigh**ty**
…-…	twenty**-**two, twenty**-**three, …	

6 **Verdrehen Sie die Zahlen.**

twenty-one	*21*	*12*	*twelve*
thirty-two	*32*	*23*	
thirteen			
forty-five			
seventy-eight			
ninety-four			

7 Ordnen Sie zu. Zwei der Beispiele rechts passen nicht.

1 wine.online.co.uk
2 wine-online.co.uk
3 wine_online.co.uk
4 wine@online.co.uk

a Wine hyphen online dot see oh dot you kay
b Wine online all in one word dot see oh dot you kay
c Wine at online dot see oh dot you kay
d Wine underscore dot see oh hyphen you kay
e Wine dot online dot see oh dot you kay
f Wine underscore online dot see oh dot you kay

8 Who wants to be a millionaire?

English for eXperts

1 What is 15?

a nine plus three
b eighteen minus four
c sixteen minus two
d three plus twelve

2 Harry's phone number is …

a twenty-one eighty-three seven
b two hundred and eighteen thirty-seven
c two one eight, three seven
d two eighteen thirty-seven

3 Find the 'odd one out'.

a dot
b button
c slash
d underscore

4 What's *"Milliardär"* in English?

a billionaire
b milliner
c millionaire
d millipede

!
Million = million
Milliarde = billion

The Real Thing

Australian Government
Department of Immigration and Multicultural and Indigenous Affairs

Application to visit Australia for tourism
or other recreational activities

1 How long do you wish to stay in Australia?

- Up to 3 months ☐
- Up to 6 months ☐
- Up to 12 months ☐

Your details

2 Name(s) as shown in your passport

Family name

Given names

Other names you are, or have been, known by
(including name at birth, previous married names, aliases)

3 Sex Male ☐ Female ☐

4 Date of birth DAY / MONTH / YEAR

If you are 70 years or over, you will be asked to provide evidence from your doctor that you are fit to travel and show that you have medical insurance to cover your stay in Australia. Please contact an Australian overseas mission for further advice before lodging your application. If additional medical consultations are required, a decision on your visa application will be delayed.

5 Marital status

Married ☐ Engaged ☐ De facto ☐ Separated ☐ Divorced ☐ Widowed ☐ Never married ☐

6 Place of birth Town/city Country

Ordnen Sie die roten Begriffe im Einreiseformular den deutschen Übersetzungen zu.

Antrag	*application*
Freizeitaktivitäten	*recreational activities*
bleiben, aufhalten	*stay*
bis zu	
Geschlecht	
Familienstand	
verheiratet	
verlobt	
(eheähnliche) Lebensgemeinschaft	*De facto*
getrennt	
geschieden	
verwitwet	
unverheiratet	
Geburtsort	

up to: bis zu; engaged: verlobt

My Portfolio

Lerntipps rund ums Englischlernen

Tipp 1: Allgemein

Legen Sie sich Ihren eigenen „Stundenplan" fest, sodass Sie feste Zeiten für das Englischlernen haben. Beachten Sie dabei, dass Sie lieber zwei- bis dreimal eine Lerneinheit einplanen sollten als nur einmal die Woche für ein paar Stunden.

Tipp 2: Neue Vokabeln

- Ähnlichkeiten und Gegensätze miteinander verbinden, z. B. *daughter – son*
- „Word spiders" anfertigen

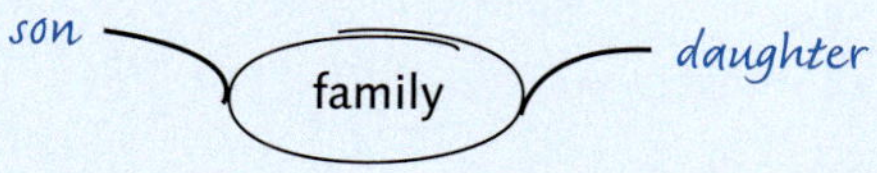

- Versuchen Sie dann, aus den Wörtern einen Text oder eine kleine Geschichte zu machen.
- Assoziationen bilden, alle Wörter aufschreiben, die Ihnen z B. zum Thema „Urlaub" einfallen.
- Vokabeln immer mit einem Beispielsatz lernen, da einige Wörter unterschiedliche Bedeutungen haben können.
- Eine „Lernkartei" anlegen (vgl. Unit 5: *My Portfolio*).
- Ein klassisches Vokabelheft anlegen: Eine Hälfte Deutsch und die andere entsprechend auf Englisch.
- Eselsbrücken bauen, denn je übertriebener und „merk-würdiger" Ihre Bilder sind, desto besser werden Sie sich das schwierige Wort merken können, z. B. das Wort *chat* = plaudern, schwätzen: Du plauderst mit Freunden im *Chatroom*.

Tipp 3: Grammatik

- Machen Sie sich mit der grammatischen Terminologie vertraut, die Sie in der Grammatikübersicht finden, dann verstehen Sie grammatische Erklärungen im Unterricht und in Büchern besser.
- Versuchen Sie selbst grammatische Regelmäßigkeiten zu entdecken und zu formulieren, denn was Sie sich selbst erarbeitet haben, bleibt besser im Gedächtnis haften.
- Merken Sie sich sog. *keywords*, die Ihnen sofort signalisieren, dass Sie eine bestimmte Regel anwenden müssen.

Tipp 4: Lernorganisation

Wie möchte ich vorgehen, um Vokabeln, Redewendungen, Grammatik, Hörverstehen etc. zu lernen bzw. zu wiederholen?

Beantworten Sie sich nun selber folgende Fragen zu Ihrer eigenen Lernorganisation:

- Welche Hilfsmittel benötige ich (z.B. Wörterbuch)?
- Wo lerne ich das, was ich lernen will, am besten (z. B. Vokabeln im Bus, im Garten)?
- Welches ist der beste Wochentag und die beste Tageszeit, um das zu lernen? Wie viel Zeit plane ich dafür ein? Wie wichtig ist es mir?
- Welche Person sollte ich mit einbeziehen (z. B. Mitlernende, Partner, Kinder)?

Legen Sie zur Kontrolle eine entsprechende Tabelle an:

Was üben	Wie?	Wann?	Wie lange?	Erledigt (✔)

3 People in my life

Vocabulary & Phrases

1 **Ordnen Sie zu.**

1	How are you?	a	Yes, that's right.
2	What's the problem?	b	Yes, here you are.
3	Who was that?	c	I'm OK. And you?
4	Who is who?	d	My boss, but don't worry.
5	Can I have a glass of wine, please?	e	Well, this is my sister Angela.
6	Is Jenny your wife?	f	We're late!

2 **Kreuzen Sie die richtige Lösung an.**

1 I'm often late
- ☐ at the morning.
- ☒ in the morning.

2 Can I have
- ☐ a glass water, please?
- ☐ a glass of water, please?

3 Winston is
- ☐ on the phone in his office.
- ☐ at the phone in his office.

4 My wife
- ☐ works by a bank.
- ☐ works for a bank.

5 Is this beautiful person
- ☐ a member of your family?
- ☐ a member in your family?

6 This is
- ☐ a photo from my brother and his family.
- ☐ a photo of my brother and his family.

3 **Finden Sie Wortpaare.**

article bad big magazine daughter sing good ~~husband~~ son colleague little boss song ~~wife~~

husband & wife

Grammar

Remember Fragewörter

who?	=	*wer?*	**Who** is it? – It's Ben.
where?	=	*wo?*	**Where** is he? – He's in the café.
what?	=	*was? wie?*	**What**'s his surname? – It's Murphy.
how?	=	*wie?*	**How** are you? – I'm fine, thanks.

4 Beginnt die Frage mit *who* oder mit *where*? Kreuzen Sie an.

	Who	Where	
1	☐	☒	... are you? – I'm on my way to work. Phone me again later.
2	☐	☐	... is Fernando Alonso? – A Formula 1 star.
3	☐	☐	... is the computer expert, Franz or Sabine? – Sabine.
4	☐	☐	... is the boss? – In his office.
5	☐	☐	... is Anna? – She's away on business.
6	☐	☐	... is Tara's partner? – Steve. He's a teacher.

!
English German
who? wer?
where? wo?

5 Ergänzen Sie das richtige Fragewort.

1 *How* are you? – I'm fine, thanks.

2 Sorry, ________'s your name again? – It's Schmitz.

3 ________ is the person in this photo here? – Oh, that's my father.

4 ________'s the boss today? – She's away on business.

6 Ersetzen Sie das Wort in Rot durch das entsprechende Pronomen.

1 Ben is in the *First Choice Café*. *He*

2 My parents live in Florida. ________

3 Susanna has a son and a daughter. ________

4 Peter and Alice are not married. ________

5 My husband and I work for the government. ________

6 Are you and Ann from the same city? ________

7 Markieren Sie *'s*, wo es für *is* steht.

Ben's not in his office. He's in the café. It's Serena's café.
Ben's boss, Mrs Morgan, is on the phone. She's in Ben's office.
Winston's in the office, too. He's Ben's colleague.

!
I'm Ben's colleague.
Ich bin Bens Kollege.
He's in the café.
Er ist im Café.

Remember **Pronomen** ***(pronouns)***

I am	**you** are	**he** is	**she** is	**it** is	**we** are	**you** are	**they** are
my name	**your** name	**his** name	**her** name	**its** name	**our** name	**your** name	**their** name
mein …	*dein/Ihr …*	*sein …*	*ihr*	*sein*	*unser*	*euer/Ihr*	*ihr*

8 Ergänzen Sie den Text mit Ausdrücken aus dem Kasten.

are • her • his • ~~is~~ • it's • our • she's • their • they're • we're

This *is* a photo of Pavel. Pavel and I ___ [1] partners. ___ [2] in business together. The name of ___ [3] company is 'Morning Glory'. ___ [4] a software company. Pavel's from Sofia in Bulgaria. I was there last year. ___ [5] parents are the owners of a hotel. ___ [6] nice people. ___ [7] daughter is a computer expert too. ___ [8] name is Reni. ___ [9] very nice too.

9 Schauen Sie sich die Tabelle an. Beantworten Sie die Fragen mit *Yes, he/she is* oder *No, he's/she's not* bzw. *No, he/she isn't.*

	Eliza	Barbara	Richard
Partner	Warren	Jim	Ann
Home	London	Scotland	Manchester
Job	pilot	teacher	magazine journalist
Hobby	volleyball	piano	tennis
Children	William, Toby	Martin, Emma	Eliza, Barbara

1. Is William Barbara's son? *No, he's not. He's Eliza's son.*
2. Is Richard Ann's husband? ___
3. Is he a teacher? ___
4. Is Emma Martin's sister? ___
5. Is Barbara a teacher? ___
6. Is Toby Martin's brother? ___

HA

Remember **Fragen und Antworten**

Frage	Kurzantworten
Is he Barbara's son?	Yes, **he is**. / No, **he's not**. / No, **he isn't**
Is she a teacher?	Yes, **she is**. / No, **she is not**. / No, **she isn't**.

Ergänzen Sie die Fragen. Verwenden Sie in Ihren Fragen die Wörter in Klammern.

7 (father) *Is Richard Emma's father?* ______ No, he isn't. He's her grandfather!

8 (journalist) ______ Yes, he is. He's a journalist for a magazine.

9 (tennis player) ______ No, she isn't. Her hobby is volleyball.

10 (son) ______ No, he's not. He's Barbara's son, not Eliza's.

11 (pilot) ______ Yes, she is. She's a helicopter pilot.

12 (married) ______ Yes, she is. Her husband's name is Warren.

Remember **Die einfache Gegenwart *(simple present)***

I / You / We / They	live, work, play, have
He / She / It	live**s**, work**s**, play**s**, ha**s**

10 **Machen Sie vier Aussagen über Eliza. Verwenden Sie die Verben *live, work, play, have*.**

1 Eliza *lives* in London. She ______ for easyJet. She ______ volleyball, and she ______ two children.

Schauen Sie sich die Tabelle in Übung 9 noch einmal an. Machen Sie vier Aussagen über Barbara und Richard in vollständigen Sätzen.

2 Barbara ______

3 Richard ______

Mixed Bag

11 Ordnen Sie die Sätze zu einem Dialog.

___ Warren. He's from Canada.
___ Toronto.
___ What's his name?
___ Oh, and where in Canada?
_2_ My sister, Eliza and her husband.
___ That's a great city.
___ Yes, but they live here in London.
_1_ Who's this?

12 Lesen Sie die Sätze und lösen Sie das Rätsel. Wohin gehört welcher Name?

Angela is married to Michael.
Michael and Angela's son is Peter.
Peter's mother is a school teacher.
Christine is Wayne's wife.
Ian and Evelyn have two daughters.
The school teacher's sister is Christine.
Emma is Peter's sister.
Wayne and Christine have two sons.
Tom has a brother.

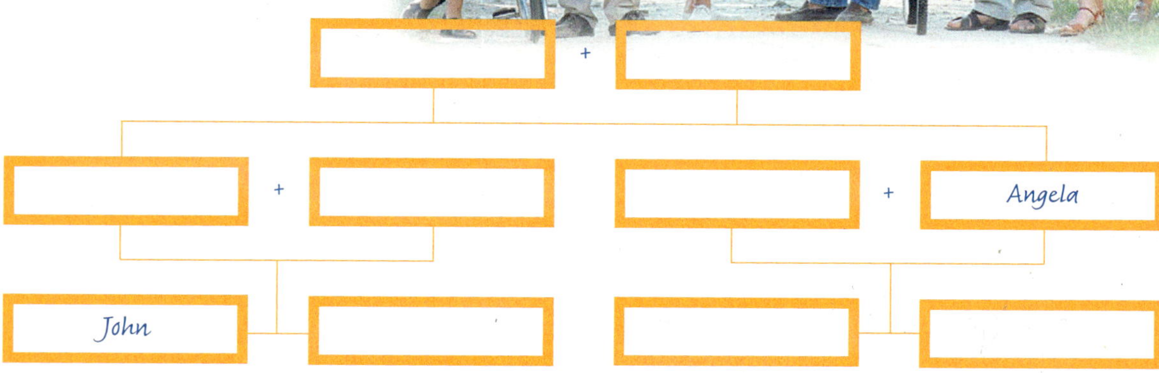

13 Lesen Sie die Visitenkarten und beantworten Sie die Fragen.

FRANK BAKER
FASTLANE
Wellington, New Zealand
f.baker@fastlane.nz
Phone: +64 (0) 4 - 57 89 65 42

Jennifer Hornby
ADWORLD
San Francisco, USA
j.hornby@adworld.com
Phone: +1 (0) 415-913 74 21

DIANA MORROW
MedAid
Bath, England
d.morrow@medaid.co.uk
Phone: +44 (0) 1225-842 842 70

1 Where is Jennifer's company? *San Francisco*
2 Who works for FastLane? ______
3 Where are MedAid's offices? ______
4 Who lives in England? ______
5 Where is Wellington? ______
6 Who is from San Francisco? ______

English for eXperts

14 Lesen Sie das Telefongespräch. Entscheiden Sie, ob die Ausssagen richtig oder falsch sind.

JESSICA Aston Hotel London, Jessica Walton, good morning.
HANNAH Hello Jessica, this is Hannah.
JESSICA Oh, hello Hannah. Nice to hear from you. How are you?
HANNAH Great, thanks. I have a new job. I work in an office now.
JESSICA That's wonderful! Where is the office?
HANNAH In Glasgow. It's quite near our home.
JESSICA What's the name of the company?
HANNAH Its name is Spectrum. It's a call centre.
JESSICA Really? What are the working hours?
HANNAH Four hours a day. It's a part-time job and I work in the evening when my husband is at home with the children.
JESSICA How many people work there?
HANNAH I have twenty colleagues in my office and there is Mr Bentley.
JESSICA Who is Mr Bentley?
HANNAH He's my boss. By the way, can I book a single room for him at your hotel?

	true	false	
1	☒	☐	Jessica works in a hotel.
2	☐	☐	Spectrum is in Edinburgh.
3	☐	☐	Hannah has a full-time job.
4	☐	☐	Hannah's husband works in the evening.
5	☐	☐	Twenty-two people work in her office.
6	☐	☐	Mr Bentley is Jessica's boss.

The Real Thing

"It runs in the family"[1]

This is the title of an American film about a busy New York family, the Grombergs. In this film we learn about the problems and conflicts between the characters. But in the end the family comes together again. Three generations of Michael Douglas' family act side by side in this film.

An interview with Michael Douglas:

Is this a film about the Douglas family?
No, it isn't. But I think the Douglas family plays the Gromberg family members very well. I really like the film very much.

What did you like about working with your dad?
In the past, my father was sometimes nervous and angry. But working with him now was so pleasant. And I also admired his work discipline.

Do you think you are out of your father's shadow now?
Well, yes, with the Oscar for "Wall Street" I felt that I finally made it.

What do you and your father have in common?
I think I have his strong will and his endurance. Unfortunately, I get sometimes angry, too.

And what has your son Cameron inherited from you?
I don't know. He has a big talent as a disc jockey – but not from me! I like music, but it's not in our family. I think he's still very young and when you are the son or daughter of successful parents it takes longer to find out who you are.

1 **Welches Talent hat Michaels Sohn Cameron nicht von seinem Vater geerbt?**

[1] Deutscher Titel: „Es bleibt in der Familie", eigentlich: Es liegt in der Familie.

busy: beschäftigt; conflicts: Konflikte; between: zwischen; side by side: Seite an Seite; well: hier: gut; really: wirklich; sometimes: manchmal; angry: zornig, wütend; pleasant: angenehm; (to) admire: bewundern; discipline: Disziplin; shadow: Schatten; felt: (to) feel: fühlen, empfinden; in common: gemeinsam; strong will: starker Wille; endurance: Ausdauer; unfortunately: unglücklicherweise; inherited: (to) inherit: erben; successful: erfolgreich; takes: (to) take: dauern; (to) find out: herausfinden

My Portfolio

1 **Sie besuchen einen englischen Pub, kommen mit Ihrem englischen Tischnachbarn ins Gespräch und stellen Ihre Familie vor.**

Finden Sie ein Familienfoto aus Ihrem Fotoalbum, auf dem viele Familienmitglieder zu sehen sind. Kleben Sie das Foto auf ein leeres Blatt und beschriften es.

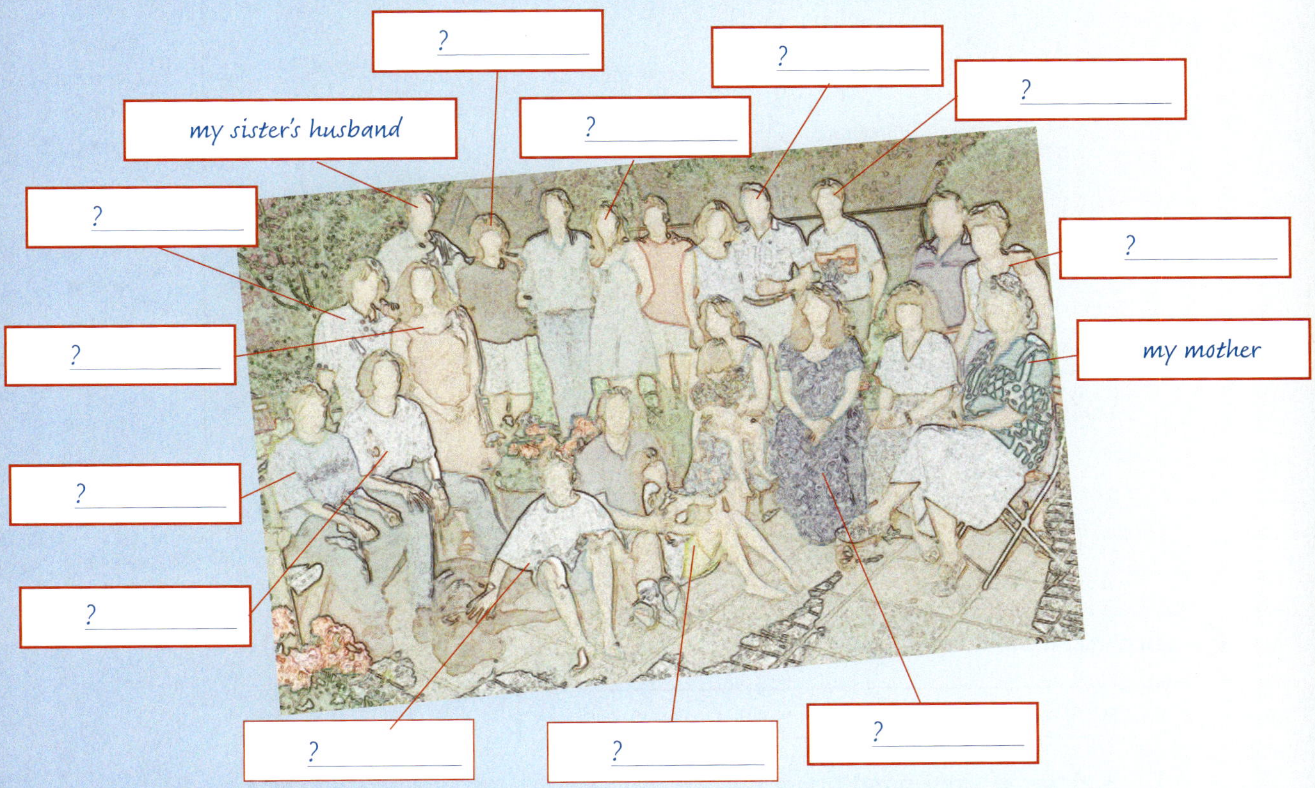

2 **Ihr Tischnachbar ist neugierig geworden. Erzählen Sie mehr über die Personen auf dem Foto (Wo wohnen sie? Wo arbeiten sie? Wie alt sind sie? etc.).**

My uncle works for a computer company.

...

3 **Sie möchten mehr über Ihre/n Kursleiter/in erfahren. Welche Fragen könnten Sie ihr/ihm über ihre/seine Familie stellen?**

What is your sister's first name?

...

4 My favourite restaurant

Vocabulary & Phrases

1 **Sortieren Sie die rechts stehenden Begriffe in die Speisekarte ein.**

F·I·R·S·T C·H·O·I·C·E C·A·F·É

Menu

Main courses _Pizza_ margherita (________ and ________)

Hamburger and ________

________ curry

________ nuggets

Or try one of our ________ or help yourself from the ________ bar.

Desserts ________ mousse

________ salad

Drinks ________ and ________

________ (Vittel)

cheese
chicken
chips
chocolate
coffee
fruit
mineral water
~~pizza~~
salad
sandwiches
tea
tomato
vegetable

2 **Ergänzen Sie das fehlende Wort.**

about • at • by • for • ~~of~~ • on • out • round

1 A **glass** _of_ **red wine**, please.

2 I'm Anita, ______ **the way**.

3 The customer ______ **the other table** is ______ **the phone**.

4 I don't like pizza. **What** ______ **you**?

5 I'd like to go ______ **the world**.

6 Can you **find** ______ the exact address ______ me, please?

3 **Bringen Sie die Ausdrücke in eine logische Reihenfolge.**

I don't like

I hate

I love

I like

I quite like

Grammar

!
He like**s** it.
He **doesn't like**.
He ~~doesn't likes~~

Remember **Die Verneinung der einfachen Gegenwart**

Bejaht	I / You / We / They	**like** it.	He / She / It	**likes** it.
Verneint	I / You / We / They **don't**	**like** it.	He / She / It **doesn't like**	it.

4 **Was mag Paul? Ergänzen Sie *I like* oder *I don't like*.**

I like

I don't like

curry	fast food
German wine	warm beer
luxury hotels	airports
music	mobile phones

1 *I like* German wine.

2 *I don't like* airports.

3 ______ curry.

4 ______ Beethoven.

5 ______ warm beer.

6 ______ hamburgers.

7 ______ Riesling.

8 ______ mobile phones.

Und nun beraten Sie Ann.

ANN Where can I go with Paul?

YOU You can't go to McDonald's because he *doesn't like* fast food.

But you can go to an Indian restaurant because he ______ 1 curry.

ANN There's a new Indian restaurant at the airport. Is that OK, do you think?

YOU No, sorry. He ______ 2 airports. But he ______ 3 luxury hotels.

ANN I'm not a millionaire! No, we can't go to a luxury hotel. What about a wine bar?

YOU Yes, he ______ 4 wine.

ANN Or a piano bar?

YOU He ______ 5 music.

ANN Or a pub with live music?

YOU Well, he drinks beer, but he ______ 6 warm beer.

5 Ergänzen Sie mit den passenden Verbformen.

Moira and Bernd *live* (live) in Leipzig. They ________[1] (have) an Irish pub there. Moira ________[2] (come) from Ireland. She and her husband ________[3] (work) hard, they ________[4] (not have) much free time. The pub ________[5] (not have) a lot of Irish customers, but the German customers ________[6] (like) the Irish beer and the Irish music. Bernd ________[7] (speak) English, but he ________[8] (not speak) Irish. Moira ________[9] (speak) Irish, English and German. The children ________[10] (not speak) much Irish.

Remember **Fragen und Antworten in der einfachen Gegenwart**

Aussage	Frage und Kurzantworten
I/You/We/They **live** here.	**Do** I/you/we/they **live** here? Yes, I/you/we/they **do**. / No, I/you/we/they **don't**.
He/She/It **lives** here.	**Does** he/she/it **live** here? Yes, he/she/it **does**. / No, he/she/it **doesn't**.

6 Wie lauten die Fragen? Verwenden Sie *do*.

A Where *do you come* (you/come) from, Moira?
B Ireland.
A Oh, Ireland.
B Yes, but I live here in Germany now.
A And ________[1] (you / like it) here?
B Yes, I do. It's a great country.
A Do you have family here? Are you married?
B Yes, I am. My husband, Bernd, is German.
A And ________[2] (you / have) children?
B Yes, I do. I have two daughters.
A So, ________[3] (they / speak) English and German?
B Yes, they do.
A And where ________[4] (you / live)? Here in Frankfurt?
B No, in Leipzig.
A ________[5] (you / like it)?
B Yes, I do. Very much.

Mixed Bag

7 Was mag Jenny gerne und was nicht. Und Sie? Unterstreichen Sie die Antwort, die Ihrem persönlichen Geschmack entspricht.

INTERVIEWER Do you like Italian spaghetti?

JENNY Oh yes, I do!

YOU *Me too. I love spaghetti. / I don't.*

INTERVIEWER And what about French cheese? Do you like it?

JENNY: Oh yes, ____________ [1].

YOU: *I don't. / Me too.*

INTERVIEWER Do you like English tea?

JENNY ________, ____________ [2]. I never drink tea. I prefer coffee.

YOU *I do. / Me neither. I don't drink tea.*

8 At the market

English for eXperts

TIM Hello, I'd like a cucumber, please.

ASSISTANT Here you __are__, sir.

TIM Thank you. And a pound ________ [1] carrots, please.

ASSISTANT Anything else?

TIM Em …, oh yes, ________ [2] you have fish, too?

ASSISTANT Yes, what ________ [3] you like?

TIM Smoked salmon.

ASSISTANT How ________ [4] would you like?

TIM 300g, please.

ASSISTANT Anything else?

TIM That's all, ________ [5]. How much is that?

ASSISTANT That's ten pounds, ________ [6].

TIM ________ [7] you are. Do you know where I can get Japanese ________ [8] and nori?

ASSISTANT ________ [9] an ________ [10] shop in Manchester Road.

of
much
There's
please
do
would
thanks
Asian
Here
rice

Tim would like to prepare Japanese s _ _ _ _ [11] for his colleagues!

The Real Thing

Pubs in Britain

When you are a tourist in Britain it is often difficult to find a restaurant but there are over 30,000 pubs! A 'Pub Guide' can help you to find a good pub. It tells you where you can eat or find your favourite beer. Of course, you should go to a traditional pub. There is no waiter or waitress - you buy your drinks at the bar. You can order a simple meal, for example ploughman's lunch or jacket potatoes. A lot of pubs offer typical English specialities, too. Have a pint or half-pint of lager, bitter or ale. Since November 2005, pubs may now open 24 hours a day. Cheers!

"The Bear" is the oldest pub in Oxford. It is a small traditional pub that serves a variety of beers, wines and spirits as well as pub food such as burgers, chips, sandwiches and baguettes. Catering for vegetarians is also provided. Food is served from 12.00-3.00. No music, no games machines, just a small pub with a big welcome!

The Bear
6 Alfred Street
Oxford City Centre
Oxford OX1
Telephone
+44 (0) 1865 721783

The "White Horse" is a traditional English pub. It is 400 years old. It serves a variety of beers, wines and spirits as well as a selection of traditional English dishes. Hot filter coffee is served until 17.00.

The White Horse
52 Broad Street
Oxford City Centre
Oxford OX1
Telephone
+44 (0) 1865 728318

Beantworten Sie die Fragen:

1 Where can you eat traditional English food?
2 At which pub can you have vegetarian meals?
3 Where can you have lunch?
4 Which pub serves coffee?

favourite: Lieblings-; simple meal: einfache Mahlzeit; ploughman's lunch: Imbiss aus Käse und Brot (evtl. mit Bier); jacket potatoes: (in der Schale) gebackene Kartoffeln; pint: 1 pint = 0,57 Liter, hier: ein Glas; lager: helles Bier; bitter: halbdunkles Bier; ale: helles oder braunes Bier; oldest: älteste; chips: Pommes frites; sandwich: Sandwich, Stulle; vegetarian: Vegetarier; games machine: Spielautomat; variety of beers: Vielfalt an Biersorten; selection: Auswahl; dish: Gericht; filter coffee: Filterkaffee

My Portfolio

1 Überlegen Sie, in welchen der abgebildeten Länder Freunde, Bekannte, Verwandte und Kollegen im Urlaub oder auf Geschäftsreise waren. Beschriften Sie diese entsprechend und notieren Sie, welche Sprache in dem jeweiligen Land gesprochen wird.

2 Stellen Sie sich vor, dass Sie eine Freundin/einen Freund, Verwandte, eine Kollegin/einen Kollegen oder eine Geschäftspartnerin/einen Geschäftspartner zum Essen bei sich zu Hause oder im Restaurant einladen möchten. Sie sind sich aber nicht sicher, was die Person mag. Welche Fragen würden Sie stellen, um dies herauszufinden?

Do you ... ?

What's your ...?

...

3 Notieren Sie Ihren letzten großen Lebensmittel-Einkaufszettel auf Englisch. Was davon mögen Sie, was weniger und was überhaupt nicht? Kennzeichnen Sie die Lebensmittel entsprechend.

5 A typical day

Vocabulary & Phrases

1 **Bringen Sie diese Begriffe in eine logische zeitliche Abfolge. Schreiben Sie die Ziffern 2-10 in die Kästchen.**

___ drink coffee in the morning break

1 get up at 6.30

___ go to bed

___ have breakfast on the way to work

___ have lunch in the canteen

___ have the evening meal

___ sleep till morning

___ start work again

___ take an afternoon nap

___ watch TV till midnight

Und nun bringen Sie diese Uhrzeiten in die richtige Reihenfolge. Tragen Sie die Ziffern 2-9 ein.

___ quarter to three	___ half past three	___ half past two
1 half past one	___ ten past two	___ quarter past three
___ twenty past two	___ twenty to three	___ ten to two

2 **Ergänzen Sie die Fragen. Verwenden Sie jedes Wort nur einmal.**

eat • ~~get~~ • go to • have • journey • main • shower • start • take • watch

1 When do you get up?

2 Do you ___ a ___ before or after breakfast?

3 That's long. When do you ___ work?

4 And when do you ___ your ___ meal?

5 Do you ___ TV in the evening?

6 And when do you ___ bed?

Grammar

3 Wie lauten die Fragen?

~~do~~ • have lunch • like • start work • work • work

1 What *do you do?* I'm a secretary.

2 When ______? At 8.30. I finish work at 5.00.

3 Where ______? In an office, in the middle of town.

4 When ______? At 1 o'clock, but I don't go to the canteen.

5 Do ______ at the weekend? No, I don't. I work just the five weekdays.

6 ______ your boss? Yes, I do. I have a nice boss and nice colleagues. It's a great job.

4 Machen Sie je eine bejahte und verneinte Aussage.

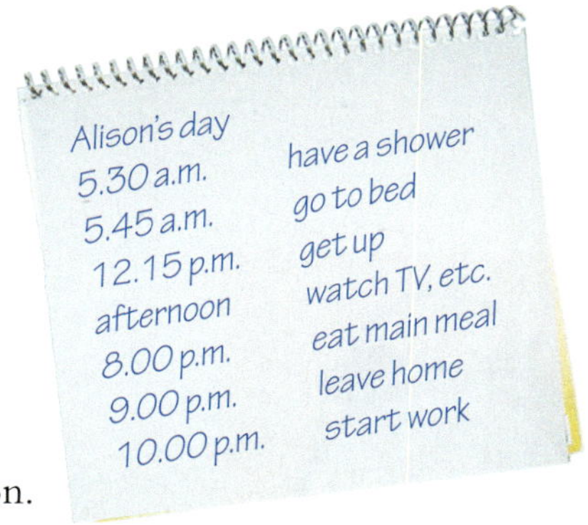

1 (have a shower) *She doesn't have a shower* before breakfast.
She has a shower after work.

2 (get up) ______ in the middle of the day.
______ early in the morning.

3 (watch) ______ TV in the afternoon.
______ midnight movies because she's at work.

4 (eat her main meal) ______ in the middle of the day.
______ before work in the evening.

5 (start work) ______ in the evening.
______ when other people start, in the morning.

What is Alison's job?

I think she is a

- ☐ system administrator
- ☐ TV presenter
- ☐ factory worker.

Mixed Bag

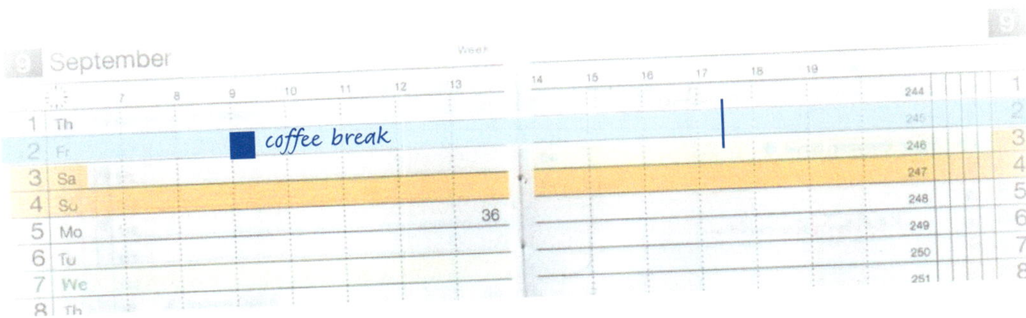

5 Ergänzen Sie mit den passenden Wörtern.

1 I get up ________ six o'clock.
on/at/in

2 I read the newspaper ________ I go to work.
at/to/before

3 Coffee break is ________ nine and quarter past nine.
from/between/at

4 I finish work at half ________ five.
to/after/past

5 I'm in the gym ________ six to seven.
at/from/between

6 In the evening my mother calls. She can talk ________ hours!
for/in/to

7 I always tell her: "Please don't call me ________ ten in the evening. I have to get up early the next morning." after/on/about

6 Wie spät ist es?

1 6.30 *It's half past six.*
2 4.40 ________
3 7.15 ________
4 22.15 ________
5 11.55 ________
6 1.30 ________
7 14.30 ________
8 9.45 ________

!
6.30 = half past six
~~half seven~~
7.30 = half past seven

7 Susan's Saturday – Vervollständigen Sie.

Every Saturday Susan gets up (get up) at eight o'clock.
Then she ________ [1] (make) breakfast.
She ________ [2] (like) tea and toast for breakfast. At nine o'clock
she ________ [3] (go) to the shops. They ________ [4] (open) at nine.
She ________ [5] (walk) there, she ________ [6] (not go) by car.
In town Susan ________ [7] (have) a snack at the market. She ________ [8] (not go)
back home for lunch. She ________ [9] (see) a lot of people at the market
but she ________ [10] (not meet) her friends there. She ________ [11] (meet) them
in the evening in a pub. But before that she ________ [12] (go) home and ________ [13] (work)
in the garden in the afternoon.

English for eXperts

8 Excuse me …

Finden Sie Ihren Weg durch das Labyrinth. Darin versteckt sich ein kurzer Dialog.
Gehen Sie jeweils ein Feld senkrecht, waagrecht oder diagonal weiter.
Tipp: Nicht alle Felder müssen verwendet werden!

Excuse	late	tell	me	between	to
me,	half	you	till	the	about
o‘clock	can	after	time,	long	p.m.
a.m.	please?	please?	past	two.	midday
before	It‘s	quarter	morning	hour	Thanks.

A Excuse me, ____?

B ____.

A Thanks.

The Real Thing

A day in the life …
… of a teleworker

Hi, I'm Stephen. I live in London and I'm a father, a househusband and a teleworker. That means that I don't go to work because my workplace is at home.
My working day is very busy. At six o'clock in the morning I feed my baby daughter Susie. My wife is not at home on weekdays. She's a flight attendant and comes back from work at the weekend.
At half past six I go into my study, switch on my computer and answer some emails. After that it's time for my first coffee. About nine o'clock I have a phone call with my boss. I always hope that little Susie doesn't start crying in the middle of it. Before midday I go shopping and after that I clean the house. I don't have lunch, I have another coffee and a snack at the computer. Between two and three in the afternoon Susie and I go for a walk in the park. I always take my mobile so my boss or my colleagues can call me for information.
I start work again in the late afternoon and finish at about half past seven. At eight o'clock I put Susie to bed. After my evening meal I look at our two clocks in the kitchen. We have a London clock and a Toronto clock because my wife works on the London-Toronto flight. When it's nine p.m. in London, she has her afternoon tea break and I can call her on her mobile phone.

Sind die Sätze wahr oder falsch?

	True	False	
1	☐	☐	Stephen works in an office.
2	☐	☐	He works from 6.30 a.m. to 7.30 p.m.
3	☐	☐	Stephen has a cat.
4	☐	☐	Stephen has lunch in a restaurant at midday.
5	☐	☐	He goes shopping in the afternoon.
6	☐	☐	Susie goes to bed at eight p.m.

househusband: Hausmann; teleworker: Heimarbeiter (per Anschluss an das Firmennetz); workplace: Arbeitsplatz; busy: beschäftigt; flight attendant: Flugbegleiter/in; study: Arbeitszimmer; (to) hope: hoffen; crying (to) cry: schreien, weinen; (to) clean: reinigen; (to) put to bed: ins Bett bringen

My Portfolio

1 Eine eigene Lernkartei erstellen

Schritt 1:
Besorgen Sie sich kleine Karteikarten (DIN A7).

Schritt 2:
Schreiben Sie alle für Sie interessanten neuen Wörter auf. Auf die Vorderseite schreiben Sie das deutsche Wort, einen Beispielsatz und zusätzlich noch vielleicht ein passendes Bild dazu. Auf der Rückseite notieren Sie die englische Übersetzung und alle Zusatzinformationen wie z.B. einen Beispielsatz, Aussprachehilfen etc.

Und so funktioniert's:

Alle neuen Karten kommen in **Fach 1**. Diese werden täglich gelernt. Wenn Sie diese können, dann wandern sie ins **Fach 2**, ansonsten bleiben sie in **Fach 1**. Wir empfehlen nicht mehr als 5 bis 10 neue Wörter pro Tag. Die Vokabelkarten in den **Fächern 2–5**, deren Anzahl immer größer wird, werden erst wiederholt, wenn diese gefüllt sind oder nach einer bestimmten Zeit, z. B. **Fach 2** nach zwei Tagen, **Fach 3** nach einer Woche, **Fach 4** nach vier Wochen und **Fach 5** nach zwei Monaten. Sollten Sie die Wörter noch immer kennen, dann wandern sie ins anliegende nächste Fach bis sie schließlich in **Fach 5** verbleiben.

2 Beschreiben Sie einen ungewöhnlichen Tagesablauf von jemanden aus Ihrem Bekannten-, Verwandten- oder Kollegenkreis: Was wird wann gemacht?

Manfred gets up at ...

6

My week

Vocabulary & Phrases

1 **Vervollständigen Sie die Namen der Wochentage und bringen Sie sie in die richtige Reihenfolge, indem Sie die entsprechende Ziffer in das Kästchen eintragen.**

___ ___ ___ ___ u ___ ___ ___ ___

___ ___ u ___ ___ ___ ___

___ ___ u ___ ___ ___ ___ ___

1 M O N D A Y

___ ___ ___ u ___ ___ ___ ___ ___

___ ___ ___ ___ ___ ___ ___ ___ ___ ___

___ ___ ___ ___ ___ ___ ___

2 **Ergänzen Sie die Sätze mit den passenden Wörtern.**

definitely • everything • actually • true • never • ~~right~~ • perhaps

1 You're a computer expert, is that right ?

2 A Who is it?

B I don't know. ______________ it's Steve.

3 The job is hard work, but ______________ I like it.

4 Do you tell your partner ______________ ?

5 I don't know why we're married. You're ______________ at home!

6 The story can't be ______________ .

7 I ______________ know the first man. He works in the bank. But who is the other person?

Grammar

Remember Die Stellung von *always*, *usually*, *often*, *sometimes*, *never*

Vor einem Vollverb	I	always/usually/often/sometimes/never	**drink** tea.
auch wenn verneint	I **don't**	always/usually/often	**drink** tea.
und in Fragen	**Do** you	always/usually/often/sometimes/never	**drink** tea?
Hinter dem Verb *be*	**I'm**	always/usually/often/sometimes/never	late.
auch wenn verneint	**I'm** not	always/usually/often	late.
und in Fragen	**Are** you	always/usually/often/sometimes/never	late?

3 Was stimmt für Sie? Wählen Sie aus jedem Satzpaar einen Satz aus und vervollständigen Sie ihn mit einem Wort aus dem Kasten.

1 I ________________ go out on Sunday evening.
I don't ________________ go out on Sunday evening.
2 I'm ________________ late on Monday morning.
I'm not ________________ late on Monday morning.
3 I ________________ get up before 6.00 in the week.
I don't ________________ get up before 6.00 in the week.
4 I'm ________________ in bed at 8.00 on Sunday morning.
I'm not ________________ in bed at 8.00 on Sunday morning.

always
usually
often
sometimes
never

! ~~I drink never tea.~~
I **never** drink tea.

4 Wohin gehört das Wort in Klammern? Kreuzen Sie die richtige Position an.

1 I ☒ go ☐ to the sauna. (often) My husband doesn't ☒ come ☐ with me. (often)
2 We don't ☐ cook ☐ lunch on Sunday. (usually) We ☐ have ☐ brunch. (usually)
3 I ☐ am ☐ at home at the weekend. (usually) But I ☐ go ☐ to the office. (sometimes)
4 I ☐ have ☐ lunch ☐ in the canteen. (never) I ☐ have ☐ only a snack. (usually)
5 My partner ☐ is ☐ up before me on Sunday morning. (often) I ☐ get up ☐ quite late. (usually)
6 Do ☐ you ☐ go ☐ shopping ☐ on Thursday evening? (always)
Is ☐ that ☐ your shopping evening? (always)

Remember Die Stellung von weiteren Ausdrücken der Häufigkeit

Meist am Satzende	I go to the gym **every day**.
	We go to bed **at 11.30**.
	Do you watch TV **in the evening**?

5 Ordnen Sie die Satzteile zu.

1 My husband usually surfs the internet — b
2 He doesn't usually go to bed
3 He often finds it hard to get up
4 We go to the pub together
5 We usually get home

a in the morning.
b every night.
c at 11 o'clock.
d before midnight.
e on Friday evening.

6 Setzen Sie die Ausdrücke in Klammern an die passende Stelle im Satz ein.

1 *I usually have the same routine in the week.*
(usually, in the week) I have the same routine.

2 ______________________________
(every day) I get up early.

3 ______________________________
(at 7.15) I leave home.

4 ______________________________
(before 8.00) I'm in the office.

5 ______________________________
(between 12.30 and 1.00) People at my office have lunch.

6 ______________________________
(often) I go shopping.

Mixed Bag

7 Was stand hier wohl zu lesen, bevor es zu regnen anfing?

1 *to* 2 ______ 3 ______ 4 ______ 5 ______ 6 ______

8 **Übersetzt man die folgenden Ausdrücke mit *in*, *at* oder *on*?**

im Winter	*in winter*	in Deutschland	______		
am Montag	______	am Wochenende	______		
zu Hause	______	in einer Besprechung	______		
bei der Arbeit	______	am Telefon	______		
am Geburtstag	______	im Urlaub	______		
auf Englisch	______	am Abend	______		

9 **See you in the pub on …**

English for eXperts

Dave, Mike und Tina haben viele unterschiedliche Berufe und Freizeitaktivitäten.
Dennoch schaffen sie es, sich regelmäßig einmal pro Woche im Pub zu treffen. Wann? Finden Sie es heraus, indem sie die Aktivitäten in die Tabelle eintragen.

Dave, Mike and Tina have full-time jobs.

Dave usually goes to the gym on Friday afternoons and sometimes also on Tuesday afternoons, but only for an hour, after work.

Mike always works very late on Mondays, but he finishes work earlier on Fridays. He always goes to the cinema in the evening.

Tina is always at home on Friday morning because she's very busy on Thursday. She usually works until seven in the evening on Thursdays and is very tired when she gets home. Late on Wednesday afternoons Mike goes to his Italian class. They sometimes go and have a pizza afterwards.

Dave always goes shopping with his wife on Saturday morning and they usually stay at home with the children for the rest of the day.

Tina always meets her boyfriend on Sundays.

	Mon	Tue	Wed	Thu	Fri	Sat	Sun
morning							
afternoon					*Dave: gym*		

Dave, Mike and Tina always meet in a pub on ______________________.

The Real Thing

What's on today?

SATURDAY Television

BBC1

5.50 PM **The Sound of Musicals**
New series 1/4. Stars of stage and screen perform
classic numbers from hit musicals of the past 75 years.
Les Misérables, Annie Get Your Gun and *Jesus Christ*
Superstar provide songs performed by David and
Carrie Grant, Jon Lee, John Barrowman – who also
acts as the backstage interviewer – Mica Paris and
Ruthie Henshall, while the team also explore the
background of the tunes. Jill Halfpenny is guest host.
Director John L Spencer; Producer Andrew Wightman (S) **496838**
Digital viewers can join in with the singalong by accessing the
on-screen lyrics available via the red button
Captain Jack of all trades: page 16; The David Butcher column: page 29; The Inside Story: page 50

6.45 Weakest Link
Lesley Garrett and Anton du Beke, Lisa Scott-Lee
and Johnny Shentall, Will Mellor and Ralf Little, and
Charles and Diana Ingram are the pairings lining up
in this special hoping to withstand Anne Robinson's
withering wit and raise cash for charity at the same time.
Series producer Alexandra McLeod; Producer Lamees Nuseibeh (S)459578
A *Weakest Link* medical special is scheduled for next Saturday,
while regular editions run Monday to Thursday at 5.15pm on BBC2

7.40 The National Lottery – Millionaire Manor
Will there be a new tenant at the Millionaire Manor?
Hosted by Mark Durden-Smith. Includes the draws.
Series director Ralph Spark; Series producer Matt Walton (S)691733

8.20 Casualty
Crossing the Line. A desperate Guppy asks Harry to
end his father's life. Bruno has a crisis of conscience.

Guppy Sandhu	**Elyes Gabel**	Luke Warren	**Matthew Wait**
Harry Harper	**Simon MacCorkindale**	Sam Bateman	**Luke Bailey**
Jas Sandhu	**Madhav Sharma**	Kenny Bradford	**Philip Middlemiss**
Bruno Jenkins	**Mark Bonnar**	Dee Bradford	**Yvonne Rochester Duncan**
Ellen Zitek	**Georgina Bouzova**	Martin Sambrook	**Eric Deacon**
Nina Farr	**Rebekah Gibbs**	Daniel Sambrook	**Tom Tyler**
Charlie Fairhead	**Derek Thompson**	Karen Sambrook	**Elaine Foster**
Tess Bateman	**Suzanne Packer**	Eleanor Sambrook	**Carol Harvey**
Maggie Coldwell	**Susan Cookson**	Tom Sambrook	**Sam Friend**
Selena Donovan	**Elizabeth Carling**	Warren Alpin	**Alex Hardy**
Kelsey Philips	**Janine Mellor**	Mary Alpin	**Maryann Turner**
Abs	**James Redmond**		

Writer Ming Ho; Producer Jane Hudson; Director Chris Lovett (S)371627

9.10 Sea of Souls

BBC2

6.30 PM **What the Papers Say**
Hosted by Krishna Guha of the *Financial Times.* **982627**
Director Vernon Antcliff; Producer Ged Clarke (S)

6.40 Flog It!
Merthyr Tydfil is the venue for the dust-'em-down-
and-price-'em-up antiques show. Presented by Paul
Martin, with experts Charlie Ross and Mark Stacey.
Series producer Peter Smith; Exec producer Tom Ware (R) (S) 431172

7.40 Some Mothers Do 'Ave 'Em
From 1973, the first ever episode of the comedy with
Michael Crawford as accident prone Frank Spencer.
Looking for a job, hapless but ever helpful Frank
attempts to become an ironmonger's salesman. **512917**
Writer Raymond Allen; Producer Michael Mills (R) (S)

8.10 Battlefield Britain
The Spanish Armada. In 1588, the English Navy
engaged in the first great sea battle in British
history when they endeavoured for 11 long days to
fend off the much bigger, more heavily armed ships
of the Spanish Armada. Experienced sailors Peter
and Dan Snow use computer-generated imagery to
re-create this landmark of maritime conflict.
Producer Nathan Williams; Series producer Danielle Peck (R) (S) (AD) 312849

9.10 Sylvia ★★★
Intimate biographical drama starring Gwyneth
Paltrow as American poet Sylvia Plath. Following a
bout of depression and a suicide attempt, Plath is
granted a scholarship to study at Cambridge, where
she meets and falls in love with fellow poet and
author Ted Hughes (Daniel Craig). **Review page 40.**

Sylvia Plath	**Gwyneth Paltrow**	Michael Boddy	**Antony Strachan**
Ted Hughes	**Daniel Craig**	Aurelia Plath	**Blythe Danner**
Al Alvarez	**Jared Harris**	Prof Thomas	**Michael Gambon**
Assia Wevill	**Amira Casar**	Morecambe	**David Birkin**
David Wevill	**Andrew Havill**	James Michie	**Julian Firth**
Tom Hadley-Clarke	**Sam Troughton**	Mr Robinson	**Jeremy Fowlds**
Doreen	**Lucy Davenport**	Myra Norris	**Katherine Tozer**

37675530
Director Christine Jeffs (2003, 15) (S) (W)
See premieres: page 36

11.00 Pleasantville ★★★★

actors
characters
comedy
documentary
feature film
lottery
press review
quiz show
TV channel

1 Sehen Sie sich diesen Ausschnitt aus einer englischen Fernsehzeitschrift einmal genau an. Können Sie die Begriffe aus dem obigen Kasten den roten Markierungen zuordnen?

2 Können Sie die nebenstehenden deutschen Begriffe zuordnen?

Filmgestalten
Dokumentarfilm
Fernsehsender
Komödie
Lotterie
Presseüberblick
Quizsendung
Schauspieler, Darsteller
Spielfilm

3 Wie lassen sich die Bewertungen der Sendungen übersetzen?

★★★★★ Outstanding ______________________

★★★★ Very good ______________________

★★★ Worth watching ______________________

★★ Could be worse ______________________

★ Poor ______________________

My Portfolio

1 Welche Freizeitaktivitäten kennen Sie?

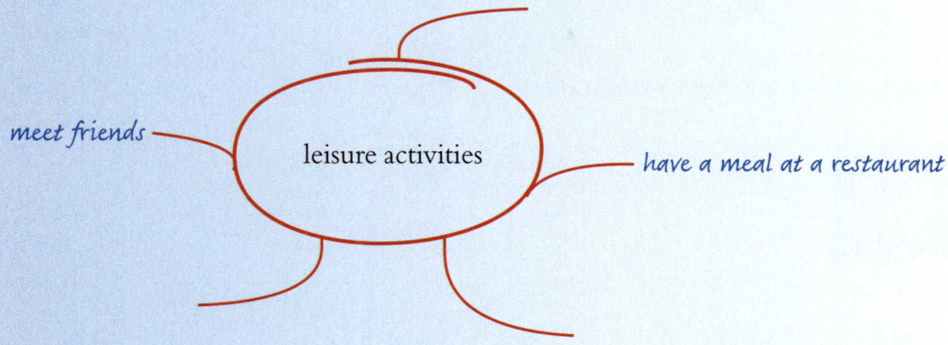

2 Wie sieht es mit Ihren persönlichen Freizeitaktivitäten aus?

What leisure activities do you *often / never / sometimes / usually / always* *do?*

I sometimes have a meal at a restaurant on Saturdays.

....

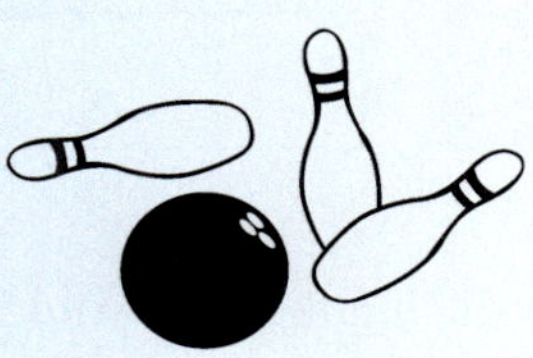

3 Was wird bei Ihnen vor Ort an Freizeitaktivitäten angeboten?

On Sunday morning at 9 o'clock you can go to church.

...

4 Welche Angebote vermissen Sie an Ihrem Wohnort?

We don't have *a/an* *internet café.*

many *gyms*

... *...*

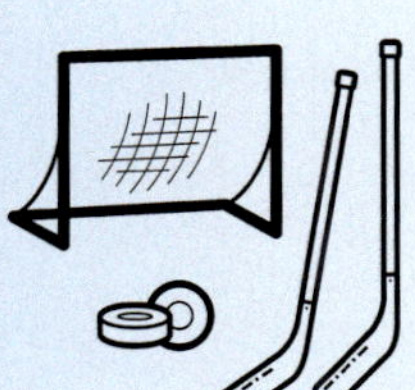

Today, yesterday & last week

Vocabulary & Phrases

1 **Ergänzen Sie das Kreuzworträtsel.**

What is the highlighted word? Clue: this is what you do with the other things: you _ _ _ _ _ _ by taxi, by ..., etc.

2 **Sortieren Sie die Zeiten ein.**

~~week~~ • 35 minutes • Sunday • two weeks • an hour • September

last *week* ______________

______________ ago

last ______________

______________ ago

last ______________

______________ ago

! vor drei Wochen
= three weeks **ago**
~~for three weeks~~

3 Ersetzen Sie die Zeitangaben in Klammern durch Ausdrücke mit *ago*.

It's Friday morning at five to twelve, and Laura Higgins is just back from a business trip. This time yesterday she was in Paris. *Two days ago* (On Wednesday) she was in Gdansk, Poland, and ________________ [1] (on Monday) she was in Leipzig, Germany. She's back in the office, and there are some messages on her answering machine. One is old – a Mr Okinawa phoned from Japan ________________ [2] (on Tuesday) – and two are new: Fernando Rodrigez phoned from Madrid ________________ [3] (at 10.55), and again ________________ [4] (at 11.45).

4 Wie lautet die Wendung mit *have*?

This is what you do when you ...

1 eat lunch or dinner. *have a meal*

2 go to Spain for two weeks. *have a* ________________

3 sit down and talk to a business partner. ________________

4 invite 20 friends on your birthday. ________________

5 go dancing with a man or woman or meet him/her for dinner. ________________

6 go to the bathroom, e.g. after a long journey. ________________

7 are thirsty. ________________

8 sit down in the garden and take it easy. ________________

Grammar

Remember **Die einfache Vergangenheit *(simple past)***

Gegenwart	Vergangenheit	
I work, he works	I work**ed**, he work**ed**	Regelmäßige Verben: + **-ed**
I say, she says	I **said**, she **said**	Unregelmäßige Verben: eigene Formen

Die Vergangenheitsform ist immer gleich (keine Sonderform in der dritten Person).

5 Und nun ergänzen Sie die Sätze.

1 My grandfather lived and _worked_ in Spain for much of his life.
2 In the last lesson we asked and ______________ questions all the time.
3 Yesterday we went to a movie. It started at half past eight and ______________ at quarter to ten.
4 I didn't know what to do. I loved him and ______________ him at the same time.
5 When I got home from Canada, I phoned and ______________ hello to all my friends again.
6 After the concert, we sat in the bar and ______________ till midnight.
7 Yesterday after work I was so tired that I just went home and ______________ TV.
8 There was a filmstar on the plane to London last week. I looked at him and I ______________, "I know that man!"
9 My birthday came and ______________, but I didn't hear from my brother.
10 We were in the restaurant all evening. We ate and ______________ and had a great time.
11 I read your message, and then I ______________ you an email. Didn't you get it?
12 Last week I lost my passport, then ______________ it again two days later!

Remember **Die einfache Vergangenheit: Verneinung**

!
I didn't know
~~I didn't knew~~

Gegenwart	Vergangenheit
I **don't** ask, he **doesn't** ask	I **didn't** ask, he **didn't** ask
we **don't** know, she **doesn't** know	I **didn't** know, she **didn't** know

Bei regelmäßigen und unregelmäßigen Verben und allen Personen immer: **didn't** + Infinitiv.

6 Ergänzen Sie die verneinte Vergangenheit eines passenden Verbs.

1 A Did you think they're nice people?
B Well, she was OK, but I *didn't like* him!

2 A And the woman next to him is his wife.
B His wife!? I ______ that he's married!

3 A Where were you?
B I'm sorry, I ______ you. There were so many people.

4 A We have to show our passports.
B Our passports? Oh no! I ______ that we would need them.

5 A Can't you see I'm busy?
B Yes, I'm sorry. I ______ to disturb you, but I need your help.

6 A I phoned him because I ______ his email address.
W I know it, but you ______ me.

Remember **Die einfache Vergangenheit: Fragen**

Gegenwart	Vergangenheit
When **do** you normally **eat**?	When **did** you last **eat**?

Bei regelmäßigen und unregelmäßigen Verben und allen Personen immer: **did** + **Infinitiv**.

!
When did you last **eat**?
~~When did you last ate?~~

7 Wie lauten die Fragen?

1 *When did you finish* (finish) work today? — At four.
2 But you arrived home at seven. Why ______ (get home) so late? — I was in town.
3 Why ______ (go) into town? — I had an appointment.
4 Where ______ (have) this appointment? — In a pub.
5 In a pub? Who ______ (meet)? — I can't answer that.
6 What ______ about (talk)? — I can't tell you. It's someone's birthday.

Remember **Die einfache Vergangenheit des Verbs *be***

Gegenwart	Vergangenheit
I **am**, he/she/it **is**	I **was**, he/she/it **was**
you / we / they **are**	you / we / they **were**

Mixed Bag

8 **"Those were the days ..."**
Setzen Sie die Verben in die Vergangenheit.

Tell me about the time when you _were_ (be) young, Grandpa.

Well, life ________[1] (be) very different, when I ________[2] (be) your age.

For example?

I ________[3] (not go) to school by bus, and I ________[4] (not have) a motorbike like your mother. I always ________[5] (walk) or I ________[6] (go) by bike. After school I often ________[7] (play) football with my friends. We ________[8] (not have) computers of course.

What about the cinema? Did you never go there?

The cinema? There ________[9] (be) no cinema in our small village. And the bus into the city ________[10] (be) too expensive. My parents ________[11] (not have) a car like your parents, you know.

But how did you go on holiday then?

We didn't! We only ________[12] (visit) our aunts and uncles from time to time. The only way to get there ________[13] (be) by train.

Poor grandpa! No computer, no cinema and no car ...

Poor grandpa? Oh no! Me and my friends ________[14] (be) very happy and we ________[15] (have) a great time together. We ________[16] (not need) your mobiles and your CDs and all these things. I ________[17] (have) lots of good friends.

By the way, how did you meet grandma?

When I was about seventeen I went dancing on Saturday afternoons. One day I ________[18] (see) this beautiful girl. But I ________[19] (not speak) to her because I ________[20] (know) she ________[21] (have) a boyfriend. But then, a long time later, someone ________[22] (tell) me that the boy ________[23] (be) her brother. I was so happy that I ________[24] (ask) her to dance with me. After that we ________[25] (go) out together every Saturday.

What a happy ending!

Lesen Sie den gesamten Text noch einmal in Ruhe auf den Inhalt konzentriert durch.

English for eXperts

9 **Eddy wird verdächtigt gestern Lady Agathas Juwelen gestohlen zu haben. Wie fragt der Inspektor im Verhör?**

INSPECTOR *Where were you yesterday, Eddy?*

EDDY I was at home.

INSPECTOR All day?

EDDY Well, no I went to the shops.

INSPECTOR *When* ______________________________?

EDDY At about ten o'clock.

INSPECTOR ______________________________?

EDDY I bought bread and cheese.

INSPECTOR ______________________________?

EDDY Then I went home.

INSPECTOR ______________________________?

EDDY I had lunch and then I slept.

INSPECTOR ______________________________?

EDDY For about three hours.

INSPECTOR ______________________________?

EDDY I got up, left the house and walked in the park.

INSPECTOR No, you didn't. You went straight to Lady Agatha's house, opened the window and took the jewellery!

EDDY I didn't open the window.

INSPECTOR Why didn't you open the window?

EDDY Because it was open already … Oops …

INSPECTOR Eddy, you are under arrest!

The Real Thing

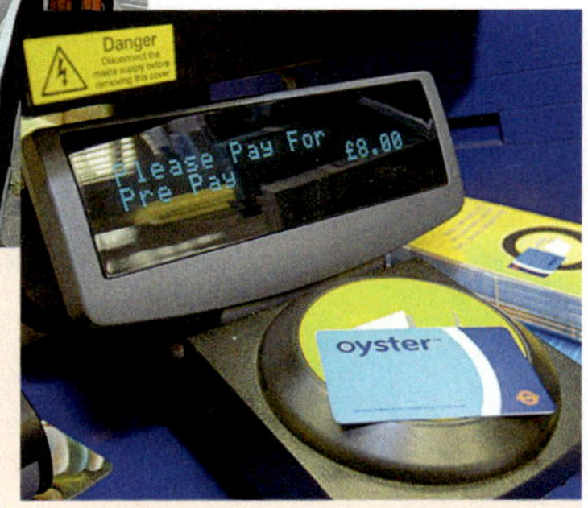

THIS IS LONDON:
7 million people,
3 million commuters daily,
273 tube stations,
145 overground stations,
7 motorways,
5 airports
... and it's still quicker to walk.

London toll

Until a few years ago driving into London's city centre by car was very difficult. The traffic was very bad. And it was very slow, only 3 miles (= 4.8 kilometres) per hour. 43% of the 22 million trips per day were by car. So there were always lots of traffic jams and people were very angry.

Then, in 2003, the city's mayor, Ken Livingstone, decided to introduce a toll. That means you must pay £8 if you drive into the city between 7 a.m and 6.30 p.m on weekdays.

You can pay at one of the 9,500 pay points or at petrol stations and shops. 230 video cameras check the cars in the toll zone, which is about eight square miles or 21 square kilometres. The money is used for public transport, for example buses and the underground. So the toll reduces the number of cars, helps the bus network and makes central London a better place for the people who live and work there and for the tourists. 90% of the people use public transport now.

But still about 40,000 vehicles an hour drive into the toll zone in the morning peak hours 7 to 10 in the morning!

Lesen Sie den Text noch einmal durch und sehen Sie sich die Bilder an. Beantworten Sie die Fragen.

1 How much is the toll?
2 Do you have to pay if you visit the city centre in the late evening?
3 How much is it at the weekend?
4 Where can you pay?
5 What is the best way to travel into London's city centre?

commuters: Pendler; tube: Röhre, Tunnel, auch Bezeichnung für die Londoner U-Bahn; overground: oberirdisch; kilometres per hour: Stundenkilometer; trips: Fahrten; traffic jams: (Verkehrs-)Staus; mayor: Bürgermeister; (to) introduce: einführen; toll: Maut, Benutzungsgebühr; pay points: Zahlstellen; petrol stations: Tankstellen; toll zone: Mautzone; square miles: Quadratmeilen; public transport: öffentliche Verkehrsmittel; reduces: (to) reduce: reduzieren; vehicles: Fahrzeuge; peak hours: Hauptverkehrszeiten

My Portfolio

1 **Stellen Sie sich vor, dass Ihre Bekannte/Ihr Bekannter, Ihre Kollegin/Ihr Kollege gerade aus dem Urlaub zurückkommt. Sie sind überrascht, da Sie das gar nicht mitbekommen haben.**

Welche Fragen würden Sie ihr/ihm über ihren/seinen Urlaub auf Englisch stellen?

Wohin? Wie lange? Mit wem? Wann? Wie? Tagesablauf?

2 **Bei einem Ihrer nächsten Besuche in einer größeren Stadt besorgen Sie sich deutsche und, falls vorhanden, englische Touristeninformationsblätter. Oder schauen einfach auf die entsprechende Internetseite der Stadt, die hoffentlich auch eine englische Version hat.**

Schreiben Sie die für Sie interessanten Sehenswürdigkeiten heraus – mindestens acht verschiedene - und lernen Sie sie mit einer der bisher vorgestellten „Lernmethoden“. Nehmen Sie ggf. ein Wörterbuch zu Hilfe.

In einer Woche überprüfen Sie selbst, an wie viele der gelernten Sehenswürdigkeiten Sie sich noch auf Englisch erinnern.

3 **Beschreiben Sie, wie Ihre Freunde, Kollegen oder Nachbarn zur Arbeit und/oder in Urlaub fahren.**

Sparren-Castle in Bielefeld

City centre of Dresden

Molecule Men in Berlin

8 From year to year

Vocabulary & Phrases

1 Beantworten Sie die Fragen.

What is the date and what do people say to you on this day?

1 Halloween is *on (the) 31st of October* and children say 'Trick or Treat' *(„Gib Süßes oder es gibt Saures")*.

2 Christmas is ____________ and people say ____________

or ____________ ____________.

3 New Year's day is ____________ and people say ____________ ____________ ____________.

4 My birthday is ____________ and people say ____________ ____________.

2 Wie lautet der Ausdruck mit *go*? Ergänzen Sie.

1 *go shopping* 

 2 ____________

3 ____________ 

4 ____________ 

 5 ____________

 6 ____________

Und wie lauten nun diese Wortverbindungen?

8	watch — g	a	a barbecue
9	buy	b	money
10	have	c	music
11	lie	d	on a beach
12	listen to	e	relatives
13	spend	f	souvenirs
14	visit	g	TV

Grammar

didn't work ~~didn't worked~~
didn't go ~~didn't went~~
wasn't/weren't ~~didn't be~~

Remember **Die einfache Vergangenheit *(simple past)***

		Verneinung
Regelmäßige Verben	I/you /he/... work**ed**	I/you/he/... **didn't work**
Unregelmäßige Verben	I/you/he/... **said/went/...**	I/you/he/... **didn't say/go**/...
Verb *be*	I/he/she/it **was**	I/he/she/it **wasn't**
	you/we/they **were**	you/we they **weren't**

3 Ergänzen Sie die Verben in der Vergangenheit.

It _was_ (be) my 30th birthday last week, and my two best friends ________ 1 (give) a big barbecue party for me. That ________ 2 (be) their present to me. I ________ 3 (think) that ________ 4 (be) really nice of them. They ________ 5 (organize) everything. I ________ 6 (not cook), they ________ 7 (plan) the food and they ________ 8 (buy) the drinks, too. I only ________ 9 (write) the invitations. So it ________ 10 (not be) a lot of work – for me. On the day of the party they ________ 11 (send) me away and they ________ 12 (get) everything ready. I ________ 13 (go) shopping (and I ________ 14 [spend] much too much money) and then I ________ 15 (sit) in a beer garden for the rest of the afternoon, while they ________ 16 (do) all the work. When I ________ 17 (come) home, everything ________ 18 (be) ready. We ________ 19 (be) a big group – over 40 people – so my friends ________ 20 (have) a lot to do. It ________ 21 (be) a warm September evening, and it ________ 22 (not rain). We all ________ 23 (have) a great time.

Remember **Fragen und Kurzantworten in der einfachen Vergangenheit**

Regelmäßige/unregelmäßige Verben	What/Where/When/... **did** you/he/... **work/go**?	
	Did you/he/... **work/go**?	Yes, ... **did**. / No, ... **didn't**.
Verb *be*	What/Where/When/... **was** I/he/she/it ...?	
	Was I/he/she/it ...?	Yes, ... **was**. / No, ... **wasn't**.
	What/Where/When/... **were** you/we/they ...?	
	Were you/we/they ...?	Yes, ... **were**. / No, ... **weren't**.

4 Bilden Sie Fragen in der einfachen Vergangenheit mit den Begriffen aus der Box.

have a good time • go to Holland again over ~~carnival~~
so what you do • what you pay
where you stay • why that • you away long

ANN *Did you go to Holland again over carnival?*

BARBARA No, we didn't. We went skiing, in Austria.

ANN ______ 1

BARBARA In Tyrol, in a holiday flat.

ANN ______ 2

BARBARA Not much. Only €45 a night.

ANN ______ 3

BARBARA Yes, we did. But we didn't do much skiing.

ANN ______ 4

BARBARA It was too warm.

ANN ______ 5

BARBARA We spent a lot of money!

ANN ______ 6

BARBARA Only from 12th to 16th of February.

Mixed Bag

5 Tragen Sie die Monate ein, die 31 bzw. 30 Tage haben.

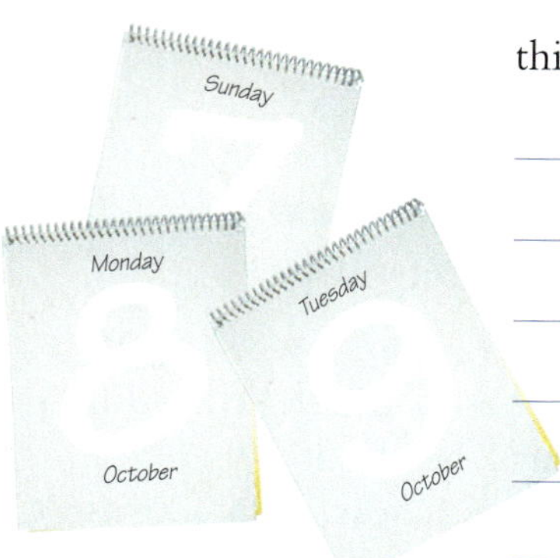

thirty-one days:

______
______
______
______
______
______
______

thirty days:

______
______
______
______

Welcher Monat hat weniger als 30 Tage?

______

6 **Wählen Sie für jeden Satz die passende Präposition aus den unten stehenden Möglichkeiten.**

1 In the Royal Hotel breakfast is ____________ seven and ten thirty.

2 I get up ____________ seven o'clock.

3 Please don't call me ____________ ten in the evening. I go to bed very early.

4 We watch television ____________ the evening.

5 Tim and Sandra don't go to a restaurant ____________ a weekday, they go there at the weekend.

6 My wife's working hours are ____________ nine to five.

7 Phone calls with my mother are very long. She can talk ____________ hours!

1	2	3	4	5	6	7
at	on	after	at	in	between	in
from	at	on	after	at	from	on
between	in	from	in	on	at	for

English for eXperts

7 **Können Sie die „Gold-, Silber- und Bronzeausdrücke" den Sätzen zuordnen?**

1 What? Sue won the *first prize* in last Saturday's lottery? That's wonderful!

2 I didn't like the film yesterday. It was really ______________________________.

3 In India, for example, English is the ______________________________.

4 You must give ______________________________ when there is an accident.

5 The "Ritz" in Paris is a ______________________________.

6 No, this is not a new car. I bought it ______________________________.

The *Real* Thing

Wer in seinem Urlaub nur Übernachtung mit Frühstück möchte, für den ist *B&B* genau das Richtige, *Bed and Breakfast*.

ORPHIR Map Ref D10 ★★★ B&B

Mrs M Wishart, Foinhaven,
ermiston Road, Stromness, Orkney KW16 3HD
/f: 01856 811249 m: 07730 386928
foinhavenbandb@orphir1.freeserve.co.uk
ww.orknet.co.uk/foinhaven/index.htm
omfortable en-suite accommodation, in a modern family me, overlooking Waulkmill Beach and Scapa Flow. Ideal se for touring. 4 miles from South Isles ferry to Hoy. Open year. Children welcome. Loch fishing nearby, boats for hire.

Single	Double	Twin	Family	En-suite	D, B&B
£30			2 £20-£25	2	

STENNESS Map Ref C9 ★★★ B&B

Mrs M C R Page, Strowan Lodge, Stenness, Orkney KW16 3JX t: 01856 850521
For the discerning guest who seeks quality of servic in a peaceful setting. Situated in the heart of Neolith Orkney, overlooking lochs Stenness and Harray. Larg garden and parking area. Not suitable for childre Open 1st April to 1st Oct.

Single	Double	Twin	Family	En-suite	D, B&B
1 £25-£35	1 £25-£35				from £37.50

OUTH RONALDSAY Map Ref G12 ★★★★ B&B

Tracey Jackson, Shoreside, South Ronaldsay, Orkney KW17 2TQ
: 01856 831560 f: 01856 831436
e: tracey@shellfish.co.uk www.orkneyholiday.com
Luxury accommodation with three en-suite bedrooms comprising two double and one family room. Superb waterside location. Evening meals prepared from the finest shellfish caught by our own fishing boat. Lobster always available.

Single	Double	Twin	Family	En-suite	D, B&B
-	2 £25-£35	-	1 £25-£35	3	from £50

F9 ★★★ B&B

Mrs J Hume, 1 Papdale Close,
Kirkwall, Orkney KW15 1QP
t: 01856 874201
Modern family home in quiet residential area, easily accessible to town centre. Close to the swimming pool.

Single	Double	Twin	Family	En-suite	D, B&B
		2 £17-£19			

Sehen Sie sich die Übernachtungsmöglichkeiten genau an. Welche würde sich für die folgenden Urlauber jeweils am besten eignen? Wichtige Begriffe finden Sie weiter unten im *B&B Dictionary*.

1. Susanne und Harald möchten gerne etwas abseits auf dem Lande übernachten.
2. Die Studentinnen Andrea und Heike suchen eine zentrumsnahe Unterkunft. Die beiden Amateurschwimmerinnen möchten auch im Urlaub fit bleiben, aber das Meer ist viel zu kalt!
3. Als passionierte Feinschmecker freuen sich Angelika und Wolfgang Neumann darauf die lokalen Meeresspezialitäten genießen zu können.
4. Der an Archäologie interessierte Geschichtslehrer Georg Heller sucht sowohl Erholung als auch die Nähe zu den jungsteinzeitlichen Stätten der Orkneys.

B&B Dictionary

accessible: erreichbar; accommodation: Unterkunft; close: nahe; discerning: anspruchsvoll; en suite: Zimmer mit eigenem Bad; ferry: Fähre; harbour: Hafen; lobster: Hummer; location: Lage; Neolithic: jungsteinzeitlich; overlooking: mit Blick hinunter auf; residential area: Wohngebiet; rural: ländlich; shellfish: Meeresfrüchte; shoreline: Uferlinie; smoke free: rauchfrei; spacious: geräumig; superb: vorzüglich; superior: gehoben; surrounding: umliegend; twin room: Zimmer mit zwei getrennten Betten

My Portfolio

1 **An welchem Datum und welchem Wochentag liegen folgende Feiertage in diesem Jahr?**

Christmas Eve	Heiligabend	*Sunday, (the) 24th December*
Christmas Day	1. Weihnachtstag	
Boxing Day	2. Weihnachtstag	
New Year's Eve	Silvester	
New Year	Neujahr	
Good Friday	Karfreitag	
Easter	Ostern	
Ascension Day	Himmelfahrt	
Whitsun	Pfingsten	
Day of German Unity	Tag der deutschen Einheit	

2 **Notieren Sie wichtige Daten in Ihrem Leben.**

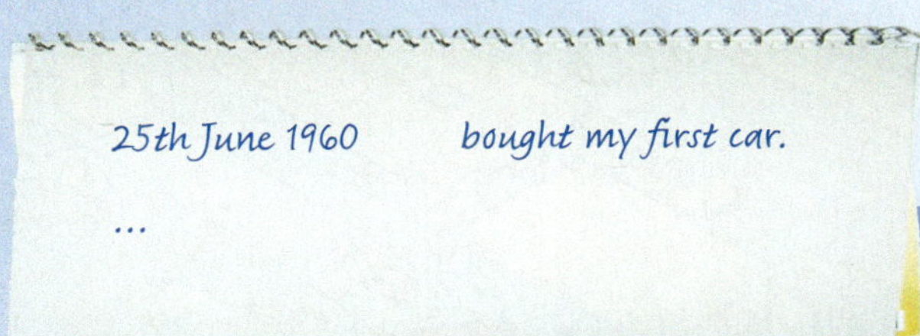

3 **Schreiben Sie einem Teilnehmer aus Ihrem Kurs eine Postkarte (oder eine virtuelle Postkarte) und berichten Sie von einem interessanten Urlaub, den Sie einmal gemacht haben.**

9 Home & away

Vocabulary & Phrases

1 **Ordnen Sie die unten stehenden Begriffe den Nummern im Bild zu.**

airport • bridge • ~~cathedral~~ • church • lake/river • mountain • museum • playground
station • tourist office

1 *cathedral* ______

2 ______

3 ______

4 ______

5 ______

6 ______

7 ______

8 ______

9 ______

10 ______

Welche weiteren Dinge können Sie auf dem Bild erkennen?

2 Wie lautet das Gegenteil? Ergänzen Sie die entsprechenden Adjektive.

1 It's not a *hot* country. The winters are very _cold_ .

2 The tourist office is in that *low* building next to the station. The ________ modern building on this side of the street is a hotel.

3 We live in the *northwest* of the city. The mountains are ________ of the city.

4 It was a *wet* afternoon with lots of rain. But the evening was ________ .

5 It isn't one of my *best* days today. It's the ________ day this week.

Welches Wort hat in etwa die gleiche Bedeutung?

6 Berlin is the (main city) _capital_ of Germany.

7 There is a (big) ________ lake near here where we go water-skiing.

8 The town has a very (famous) _w_ ____ _-k_ ________ university.

9 I have some (members of my family) _r_ ________ in Canada.

10 (The town where I grew up) My _h_ ________ town was a very small place.

3 Vervollständigen Sie das Gespräch.

died • got married • grew up • ~~know~~ • lives • met • retired • stay • was born

A So what part of Austria are you from?

B A place called Bregenz. Do you _know_ it?

A No, I'm sorry.

B It's in the west, on Lake Constance.

A Oh, Lake Constance. My grandmother ________ [1] and ________ [2] not far from there. She's German.

B Oh really?

A Yes, she ________ [3] my grandfather when he was a student. She ________ [4] in Portugal now.

B Portugal?

A Yes, after they ________ [5], he found a job with a hotel group, so they lived abroad all his working life. One of the countries was Portugal. They liked it very much, so when he ________ [6] they went and lived there. He ________ [7] two years ago, but she plans to ________ [8].

Grammar

Remember **Vergleiche**

A Smart is **cheaper than** a Mercedes. A Mercedes is **more expensive than** a Smart.
A Smart is not **the cheapest** car you can buy. A Mercedes is one of **the most expensive**.
Is a Smart **as** popular **as** a Golf? No, it's **not as** popular **as** a Golf.

Schreibbesonderheiten: big – bi**gg**er – bi**gg**est sunn**y** – sunn**i**er – sunn**i**est

Unregelmäßig: good – **better** – **best** bad – **worse** – **worst**

4 **Ergänzen Sie die richtige Steigerungsform.**

Australia is *warmer* than Britain, it is also ______ [1] (sunny). The ______ [2] (hot) part is the desert in the middle of the country. Britain's weather is much ______ [3] (bad); it's ______ [4] (wet) and ______ [5] (cool). But Britain is not so far from Germany, so flights are much ______ [6] (cheap). It's much ______ [7] (expensive) to fly to Australia. Australia is of course a much ______ [8] (large) country, but what a lot of people don't know is that Australia's population is much ______ [9] (small). There are only about 20 million people. So Britain has more people, it also has more famous old buildings. Australia's ______ [10] (famous) building is the Sydney Opera House.

Nun ergänzen Sie *as* oder *than*.

Many German tourists find Australia more interesting to visit ______ [11] Britain because it's more 'exotic' ______ [12] Europe. But the cities are usually not ______ [13] interesting.

Remember ***there is – there are; some – any***

There's a bus station.	**There isn't** a train station.	**Is there** an airport?
There are some pubs.	**There aren't any** cafés.	**Are there any** hotels?

5 Setzen Sie *there is / there are*, auch Verneinungen und Frageformen, ein.

A Where do you live?

B In a small village. *There are* only about 100 houses, and ______ [1] only about 400 people. ______ (not)[2] many young people, most are older.

A And what ______ [3] in the village? ______ [4] a shop or a school?

B Well, ______ [5] a pub in the village, but ______ (not)[6] a shop or a school. The children have to go to the nearest town, that's 15 kilometres away. And ______ (not)[7] any work in the village. People have to travel to work.

A But you work at home, is that right?

B Yes, I only have to travel when I go and see customers.

A ______ [8] other people like you?

B ______ [9] two.

Nun setzen Sie *some* oder *any* ein.

A Is it a nice place to live?

B Well, there aren't ______ [10] cinemas, or clubs or interesting museums of course. But there is ______ [11] lovely countryside.

A And why aren't there ______ [12] young people?

B There are ______ [13] young people, but there aren't many. It's because there aren't ______ [14] jobs.

Mixed Bag

6 Wie gut kennen Sie sich aus?

1 The 'Englischer Garten' is a *park* in Munich.
2 The 'Louvre' is a ________________ in Paris.
3 The 'Thames' is a ________________ in London.
4 The 'Oktoberfest' is a beer ________________ in Munich.
5 'Pont Neuf' is a ________________ in Paris.
6 'St Paul's' is a ________________ in London.
7 The 'Sahara' is a ________________ in Africa.
8 The 'Sorbonne' is a ________________ in Paris.

~~park~~
river
desert
cathedral
bridge
museum
university
festival

And did you know that …

9 Greenland is the world's *largest* island. (large)
10 the Amazon is the ________________ river in the world. (long)
11 the ________________ hotel room is at the 'Atlantis' in the Bahamas. (expensive)
12 the world's ________________ airport is in Atlanta, USA. (busy)
13 the world's ________________ pop group is still the Beatles. (famous)
14 the ________________ place in the world is in the Atacama desert in Chile. (dry)
15 the Taj Mahal in Agra is one of the world's ________________ buildings. (beautiful)

7 **Wie heißen die vier Geschwister dieser Familie, wie alt sind sie und welche Berufe haben sie?**

Marc is forty-three years old. He's the oldest brother.

The third member of the family is a female model.

The singer is younger than the politician but two years older than the model.

Claire is a teacher. She's thirteen years younger than the politician.

Pete is thirty-six years old.

Rhonda is two years younger than Pete and works for the most popular fashion designers.

Name	Marc	?	?	?
Job				
Age				

8 **Watch out!** **English for eXperts**

Finden Sie jeweils zwei Ausdrücke, die zwar gleich ausgesprochen werden, jedoch unterschiedliche Bedeutungen haben und verschieden geschrieben werden.

1 Can you _hear_ that noise, too? There must be a football match near *here*.

2 "You always ________ a lot of postcards." – "Yes, that's ________."

3 After ________ glasses of whisky, Danny and Pat decided to travel ________ Scotland together.

4 Let's ________ a nice souvenir for Mom before we say good-________ to our friends.

5 "Do you ________ the English word for 'Trinkgeld'?" – "________, I'm afraid, I don't."

6 We still have an ________ and ten minutes before ________ plane leaves.

7 Look, how beautiful! We can ________ the ________ and the ships from our hotel room window.

8 Our ________ can't go with us to Mallorca. He's allergic to the ________ there.

9 Is this the bus ________ Hyde Park? ________ tickets, please.

The Real Thing

Bodybuilder, Terminator, Governator ...

Personal background Arnold Alois Schwarzenegger was born on 30 July 1947 near Graz, Austria. In 1968, he moved to the United States and 15 years later, in 1983, became an American citizen. On 26 August 1986 he married TV journalist Maria Shriver, niece of late US President John F. Kennedy. Together they have four children: two daughters and two sons. Arnold has many nicknames. The most popul are "The Austrian Oak", "Arnie" and more now "The Governator": a play on the words "Governor" and "Terminator" (after the film).

Bodybuilding career In 1960 at the age of 14 he picked up a barbell for the first time at a local gym and became interested in bodybuilding. Since then, Schwarzenegger has won many championship titles, including "Mr Universe" (5 times) and "Mr Olympia" (7 times)! His film career began in 1977 with a bodybuilding documentary "Pumping Iron". At the age of 30 he got a "Golden Globe" as best newcomer. One year later he ended his bodybuilding career and entered the film business.

Acting career Schwarzenegger became famous for his action films in the 1980s. His first big action film was "Conan the Barbarian" (1982), followed by the technological and violent film "The Terminator" (1984) and "Total Recall" (1990). He quickly became a Hollywood superstar and "International Star of the Year" in 1985. His more recent films include the comedies "Twins" (1988), "Kindergarten Cop" (1990) and "Junior" (1994). "Terminator 2: Judgement Day" (1991) was one of the most successful films in history and brought in 500 million dollars!

Political career He left the University of Wisconsin Superior in1979 with a B.A. in Business and International Economics. Politically, he is a Republican and in 1990 George H. W. Bush asked him to become chairman of the "President's Council on Physical Fitness and Sports". During this time he travelled to all fifty states to promote fitness. In November 2003 he became the 38th Governor of California. Schwarzenegger's political views are quite controversial: he does not support gay marriages, but believes in the death penalty.

So, what's next? Who knows? Arnold Schwarzenegger is always full of surprises...

background: Hintergrund; became: (to) become): werden; citizen: (Staats-)Bürger; late: späte(r), ehemalige(r); nicknames: Spitznamen; Oak: Eiche; picked up: (to) pick up: hochheben; barbell: Hantel; gym: Sporthalle; documentary: Dokumentarfilm; technological: technisch; violent: brutal; (to) include: enthalten, umfassen; comedies: Komödien; most successful: erfolgreichste(r); B.A.: Bachelor of Arts (akad. Grad); Business and International Economics: internationale Wirtschaftslehre; chairman: Vorsitzender; Council on Physical Fitness and Sports: Berater des staatl. Programms für Sport und Fitness; travelled: (to) travel: reisen; (to) promote: fördern; political views: politische Ansichten; controversial: kontrovers; (to) support: unterstützen; gay marriages: homosexuelle Ehen; death penalty. Todesstrafe

My Portfolio

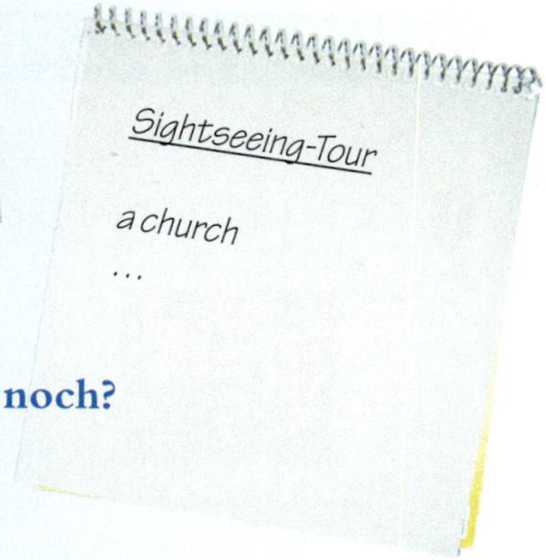

1 **An welche der Sehenswürdigkeiten aus Unit 7 erinnern Sie sich noch? Notieren Sie diejenigen auf Englisch, die Ihnen noch einfallen.**

2 **Vergleichen Sie den Ort, an dem Sie gerade sind, mit einem Ort, in dem Sie gerne Urlaub machen oder gerne Ihre Freizeit verbringen.**

My town/village is smaller than ...

3 **Beschreiben Sie die wesentlichen Lebensstationen einer Person, die Sie sehr gut kennen (Vater, Mutter, Schwester, Partnerin, Partner etc.).**

He/She was born ...

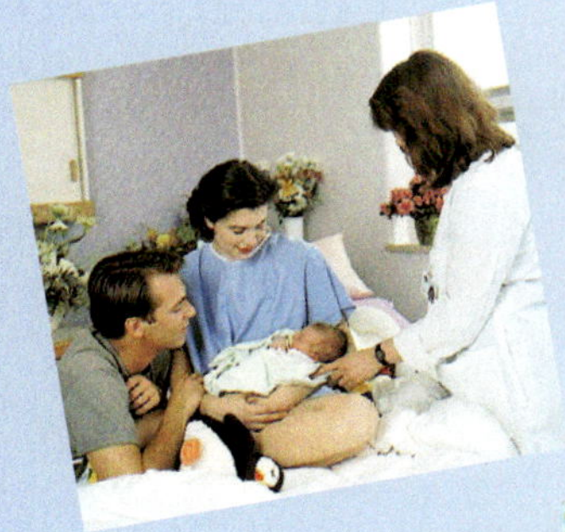

10 What sort of person are you?

Vocabulary & Phrases

1 **Wie lauten die Farben und Dinge?**

1 ______________________

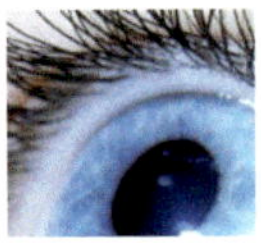

blue eye ______________________

2 ______________________

3 ______________________

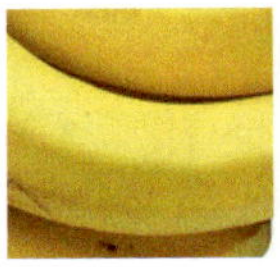

4 ______________________

5 ______________________

6 ______________________

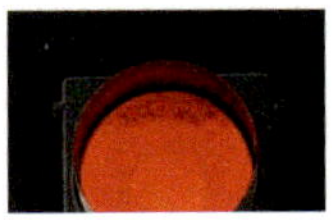

7 ______________________

2 **Bilden Sie Wortpaare aus Nomen und Verb.**

ear • ~~eye~~ • feel • fingers • hear • nose • ~~see~~ • smell • taste • tongue

1 *eye* ______________ *see* ______________

2 ______________ ______________

3 ______________ ______________

4 ______________ ______________

5 ______________ ______________

Und nun vervollständigen Sie die Sätze mit den passenden Verben von oben.

6 This coffee *tastes* and ______________ really good.

7 Sorry, I can't ______________ you very well. Can you repeat that?

8 Where were you? I didn't ______________ you.

9 I don't ______________ very well this morning.

3 Ergänzen Sie das Telefongespräch.

YOU Berger Elektronik, guten Tag.

MAN Oh, er. Hello. Do you speak English?

YOU Yes, I do. How can I help you?
Bejahen Sie. Bieten Sie Hilfe an.

MAN This is Harry Wisniewski in Chicago. Can I speak to Hannah Koch, please?

YOU 1 ______________________________
Bitten Sie um einen Augenblick Geduld.

2 ______________________________
Frau Koch ist nicht da. Sagen Sie es höflich Herrn Wisniewski.

MAN Oh.

YOU 3 ______________________________
Fragen Sie ihn, ob er eine Nachricht hinterlassen möchte.

MAN Sorry?

YOU 4 ______________________________
Fragen Sie noch einmal. Dieses Mal fragen Sie, ob Sie etwas ausrichten können.

MAN Yes, please tell her zzzzzzzzz.

YOU 5 ______________________________
Sagen Sie, dass die Leitung gestört war.

MAN Oh, well look. I think it's better if I speak to Hannah personally. I'll call back later.

YOU 6 ______________________________
Sagen Sie, dass das in Ordnung ist und dass Sie Hannah sagen werden, dass er angerufen hat.

Grammar

Remember *-ing*-Form

I like / love / prefer / enjoy read**ing**.

4 Vervollständigen Sie die Fragen.

1 How do you like spending (spend) your free time?
2 What do you like ______________ (do)?
3 Do you enjoy ______________ (listen) to music?
4 Or do you prefer ______________ (watch) TV?
5 I love ______________ (do) sports. What about you?

5 Beschreiben Sie diese Leute jeweils mit einem Adjektiv.

athletic • musical • ~~creative~~ • quiet • serious • organized • busy

1. She loves painting people and landscapes, she's very *creative*.
2. He always finds something to do, he's always ______.
3. "There's a place for everything" is her motto and she never loses anything, she's very ______.
4. He loves listening to music and enjoys playing the cello in an orchestra, he's very ______.
5. You don't hear him laughing a lot, and he's not interested in funny things, he's too ______.
6. He loves doing sports, he even runs in the London Marathon, he's so ______.
7. She doesn't speak a lot, she prefers listening, she's very ______.

Mixed Bag

6 Die folgenden beiden Personen sind ganz verschiedene Charaktere. Ergänzen Sie die Lücken mit Ausdrücken aus der jeweiligen Box.

Andrew and Christina are very different.

dancing
doing sports
listening to loud music
dynamic
comedies
working in a team
~~easy going~~
being with lots of people
walking in the rain

Andrew is a very happy and *easy-going* [1] person.
He loves funny things like ______ [2]
at the cinema and enjoys ______ [3].
He likes ______ [4] in his company.
In his free time Andrew loves ______ [5],
for example jogging.
In his music club he enjoys ______ [6]
and ______ [7] to it.
He's very ______ [8].
He even likes ______ [9]
with his dog Charlie.

Christina doesn't like ____________________[10].
She prefers ____________________[11] in front of a warm fire and she loves ____________________[12]. She's very interested in biographies. She also enjoys ____________________[13], classical not pop. Christina is not interested in ____________________[14].
She's too lazy for that, she prefers ____________________[15] on her computer. She enjoys ____________________[16], but she doesn't like big crowds in town on Saturdays.
Christina is a housewife and she loves ____________________[17], just like Mimi, her cat.

By the way, Andrew and Christina are married – to each other.

sport
sitting at home
rainy weather
surfing the internet
going shopping
being her own boss
listening to music
reading

English for eXperts

7 Bilden Sie Sätze.

Beginnen Sie jeweils mit dem nummerierten Wort und bewegen sich nach oben, unten, links oder rechts weiter.

1 I'll	2 Can	I	speak	you	want	to	leave	a
↓ give	Ms	Johnson	to	3 Do	afraid	Danny	is	message?
4 How	can	your	Danny,	please?	5 I'm	me	still	please.
6 I'll	I	message.	her	to	call	lunch?	at	manager,
call	help	you?	tell	7 I'd	back	before	school.	sales
again	later.	8 Can	you	like	to	speak	to	your

The Real Thing

Lonely hearts

WLTM good-looking, tall, clever, sporty, kind M, 40-52, f fun times & poss LTR. NW. Call Voicebox

WOMEN SEEKING MEN

●Winsome F (tall, slim, fair, 56) from Hadrian's Wall area, seeks tall, fit, h'some legionnaire (45-60 approx) with whom to engage in verbal combat. NW. Call Voicebox

●Real Russian F, 32, looking for Real M, 35-45 for an old-fashioned, romantic, honest, committed r/ship. Have British passport, like gold but do not dig. Ldn. Call Voicebox

●Coastal walking & red wine. Attract F, 43 WLTM tall dark friendly M for walking, talking, red wine, films, good company etc. Cornwall. Call Voicebox

●Attract & active, intellig, n/s F, 56, into gardening, cycling, writing, music, Italy seeks witty, kind, cultured M, sim age. Bath/Bristol. Call Voicebox

●I'm a 24 yo girl looking to meet a hot, witty, passionate M between 25-30 who are game for a laugh & a good cup of tea! Herts. Call Voicebox

●Attract vivacious F, 36, warm, intellig, life-loving, slim, sporty, into running, writing, travelling, adventures seeks fun, soulful, down-to-earth, athletic M for r/ship. Ldn. Call Voicebox

●Creative & caring F, 40s, into cinema, theatre, dance & galleries seeks kind M, 30-60, with GSOH for LTR. Ldn. Call Voicebox

●Teacher, 53, enjoys swimming & reading, music looking to meet M, 45 & 65 to see what happens... Herts. Call Voicebox

●Attract intellig F, 45, n/s, likes travel, cinema, art, seaside, good food & wine seeks honest intellig M for LTR. Brighton. Call Voicebox

●Free-thinking F, 40, seeks compassionate & intellig M. Mids. Call Voicebox

seeks sim F to share dreams. Ldn. Call Voicebox Txt

●Two goldfish in a tank...One said: 'How d'you drive this thing?!' Go on, I saw you smile. Good-looking 43 yr old seeks like. S Yorks. Call Voicebox

●Tall & attract, lovely, warm, intellig F, fun-to-be-with, young 50, worth meeting seeks tall, intellig, profess, attract M. Mids. Call Voicebox

●Attract fun F, 36 seeks profess M to pull sickies with & poss LTR. Enjoys standing at the back of gigs telling stories. Ldn. Call Voicebox

MEN SEEKING WOMEN

●Honest & caring M, 50, well-educ, 5'10, medium build, divorced WLTM kind, caring, sensitive, n/s F to share country walks, music, f/ship, laughter, conversation & who knows. Ldn/SE. Call Voicebox

●Attract & slim fit M, 48, illustrator/artist, young-at-heart, kind, honest, caring, sensitive, into dancing, cinema, galleries, travel WLTM sim attract intellig F for f/ship+. E Anglia. Call Voicebox

●Yes! Unconventional, successful businessman, 46, seeks intellig, sensual muse with good style & GSOH, up to 40. Thames Valley. Call Voicebox

●Islington M, 5'9, 53, medium build, black hair, brown eyes, good-looking, likes swimming, reading, music & yoga seeks like-minded F for companionship. Ldn. Call Voicebox

●Photographer M, 38yo, , into cinema, galleries, long walks & eating out, WLTM, F, 28/38yo, who is funny, intellig & creative for poss LTR. Ldn. Call Voicebox

●Good-looking & tall, slim, white grad profess, 47, likes salsa, tango, film, art, music, travel, the sea seeks F, any nationality, for LTR. Leics. Call Voicebox Txt

●Intellect of love. Left-wing Asian, 38, imaginative &

1 **Welche beiden einsamen Herzen könnten in Alter und Interessensgebieten wohl gut zueinander passen?**

WLTM: would like to meet; LTR: long-term relationship; F: female; n/s: non-smoker; r/ship: relationship; f/ship: friendship; M: male; GSOH: good sense of humour; profess: professional; yo: young

2 **Wem die traditionelle Kontaktanzeige zu altmodisch erscheint, der probiert es vielleicht einmal mit *Speeddating*, der Partnersuche im Schnellverfahren.**

- Do you have a busy job and very little time to go out and meet someone?
- Are you single and a bit shy, but don't want to stay alone any longer?
- Then Speeddating is perhaps the right thing for you!
- You go to a speeddating event, pay a fee and then the game starts. There are a lot of tables where men and women sit opposite each other. Then you have a few minutes together to talk about your interests and hobbies and to find out something about the other person. You get a card on which you tick boxes and take notes about your partner's characteristics and interests. Then a gong goes, and you get up and move one place. Again you have a short conversation with a new partner.
- The game organizer gets the cards and sends you an email if there is someone who liked you too and who ticked the same boxes.
- And then it's up to you …

DATE 10 PEOPLE AT ONCE

shy: schüchtern; fee: Teilnahmegebühr; (to) tick boxes: Kästchen markieren; goes: hier: ertönt; it's up to you: es liegt an Ihnen

My Portfolio

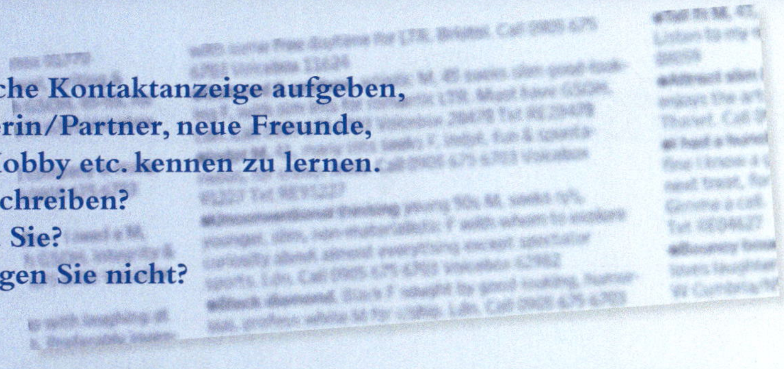

1 Sie möchten eine englische Kontaktanzeige aufgeben, um eine/n neue/n Parterin/Partner, neue Freunde, neue Bekannte für Ihr Hobby etc. kennen zu lernen. Wie würden Sie sich beschreiben? Was für eine Person sind Sie? Was mögen Sie bzw. mögen Sie nicht?

2 Listen Sie in Ihrem persönlichen Vokabelheft Ausdrücke und Redewendungen auf, die Sie zur Begrüßung am Flughafen, am Bahnhof, am Telefon oder im Hotel verwenden würden.

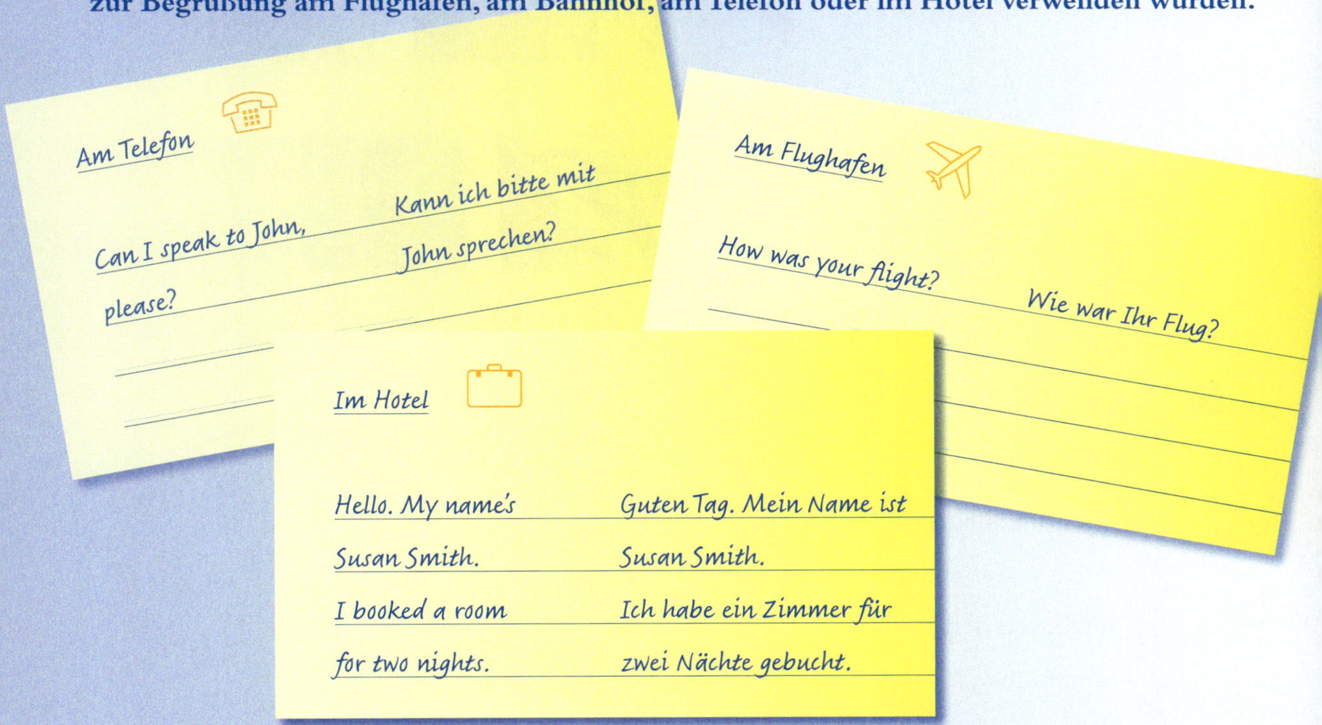

3 Hören Sie sich Ihren Lieblingssong in Englisch auf CD an und konzentrieren Sie sich auf den Text.

Schritt 1: Schreiben Sie alle Wörter heraus, die Sie verstehen.

Schritt 2: Nehmen Sie sich parallel zum Hören den Text vor. Hinweis: Die meisten Texte sind im CD-Booklet zu finden oder teilweise im Internet (Stichwort „Lyrics“).

Schritt 3: Versuchen Sie nun an Hand Ihrer Stichworte den Inhalt des Liedes zu beschreiben.

11 *Out & about*

Vocabulary & Phrases

1 **Ordnen Sie die Wörter den entsprechenden Gegenständen zu.**

~~brush~~ • comb • hairdryer • hat • sunglasses • sunscreen • walking boots

brush

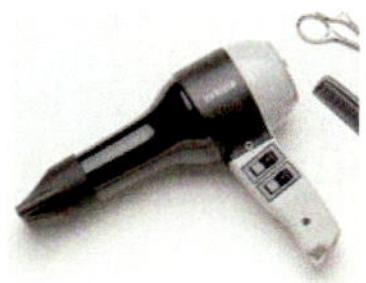

_____ 1

_____ 2

_____ 3

_____ 4

_____ 5

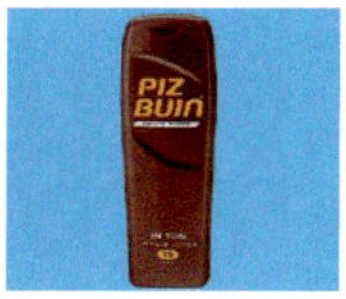

_____ 6

2 **Was ist gemeint?**

1 You need it when it rains. an *umbrella*

2 You pack and carry clothes in it when you go away. a *s* _____ *e*

3 It tells you about travel, sights, restaurants, shopping, etc. in a city or country. a *g* _____ *k*

4 It tells you all the important things you have to say as a tourist. a *p* _____ *k*

5 Your money, your passport, your credit and bank cards your *v* _____

6 Where you buy diesel for your car at a *p* _____ *s* _____

3 **Ergänzen Sie den Dialog mit *could, like, love, would*.**

A *Would* you _____ [1] to see a bit of the city?

B Yes, I'd _____ [2] to.

A Tomorrow afternoon? Is that OK?

B That _____ [3] be lovely.

A At three o'clock? Then maybe we _____ [4] have dinner together in the evening.

B Fine. See you tomorrow!

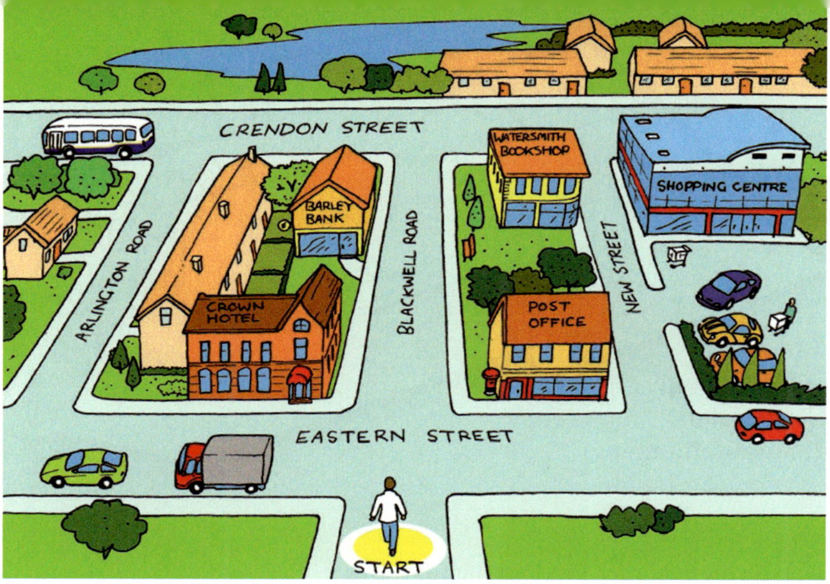

4 **Folgen Sie der Wegbeschreibung auf dem Plan.**

A Excuse me. How do I get to the shopping centre?

B The shopping centre? Well, you go along here, then turn left into Eastern Street. Go along there past the Crown Hotel. At the next junction, turn right into Arlington Road. Go along there and turn right into Crendon Street, go along Crendon Street as far as New Street. The shopping centre is on the corner of Crendon Street and New Street, opposite Watersmith's Bookshop.

Es gibt auch kürzere Wege zum Ziel. Beschreiben Sie diese.

Grammar

Remember ***will*** **zum Ausdruck von Angeboten und spontanen Entschlüssen**

Where is our hotel? – **I'll show** (~~I show~~) you on the map.
When is the city tour? – **I'll check** (~~I check~~) in the programme.

5 **Vervollständigen Sie die Angebote.**

give • help • ~~make~~ • see • take • wait

1 A I need a break. — B Good idea, *I'll make* some coffee.

2 A Can I speak to Inge, please? — B Just a moment, ________ where she is.

3 A This exercise is really difficult. — B It's OK. ________ you.

4 A I'm very sorry, but I'm not ready. — B It's OK, ________.

5 A How can I contact Wim? — B ________ you his email address.

6 A My flight is very early. — B That's OK. ________ you to the airport.

Mixed Bag

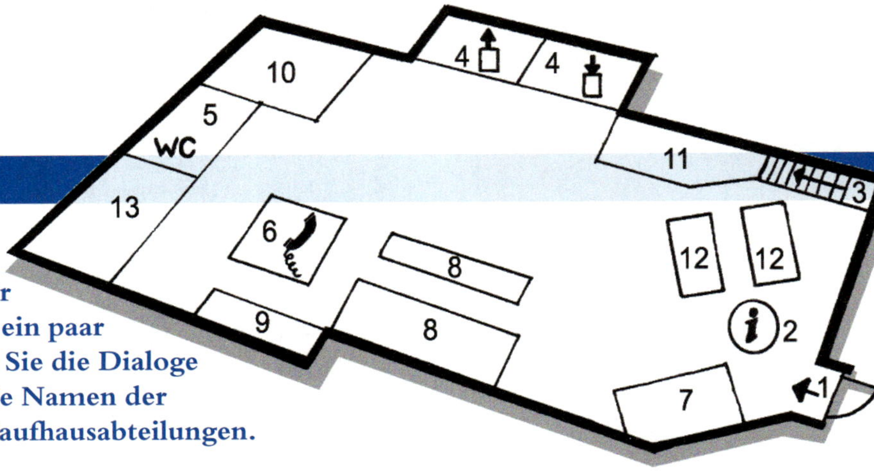

6 **Derek braucht für seine Reise noch ein paar Utensilien. Lesen Sie die Dialoge und finden Sie die Namen der nummerierten Kaufhausabteilungen.**

At the info desk:

DEREK Excuse me, can you help me? I'm looking for shoes.

ASSISTANT Certainly, sir. I'll show you the way on our floorplan. Turn right here and go through the young fashion department. The shoe department is on the left.

In the shoe department:

DEREK I think I'll take these sandals. Do you have walking boots, too?

ASSISTANT I'm afraid, we don't. But you can get them in the sports equipment department. It's just over there, next to the lifts.

In the sports equipment department:

DEREK How much are these walking boots?

ASSISTANT 87 pounds, sir.

DEREK Okay, I'll take them. They're for my hiking holiday in the Grand Canyon, you know.

ASSISTANT I see.

DEREK That's why I also need a good sunscreen.

ASSISTANT You can get sunscreen in our drugstore. Go past the toilets and turn right.

In the drugstore:

DEREK Do you know where I can buy a map?

ASSISTANT In the bookshop, sir.

DEREK How do I get there?

ASSISTANT Can you see the telephone over there? Well, the bookshop is on the right.

In the bookshop:

DEREK Where's the luggage department, please?

ASSISTANT Go along here, through toys and games and it's near the entrance.

In the luggage department:

DEREK I'd like a backpack for my holiday.

ASSISTANT I'm afraid, we only have suitcases and bags. But you can get a backpack in the sports equipment department. Let me show you on the floorplan …

DEREK I know where it is, thank you very much. Phew, well, this is a good training for my tour!

A–Z Directory

9	______
13	______
1	Entrance
2	Information
4	Lifts
7	______
11	______
10	______
3	Stairs
6	Telephone
5	Toilets
8	______
12	*Young Fashion*

English for eXperts

7 **Das Fremdenverkehrsbüro des Städtchens Bloomingdale hat sich einen Wettbewerb ausgedacht um Touristen anzulocken. Die Sehenswürdigkeiten sollen anhand des Textes richtig beschriftet werden.**

Welcome to Bloomingdale! Take a walk to the sights of our lovely town.
Our walk starts at the station (1).
Leave the station and turn left. Turn right at the Orchard Hotel (2) into Bridgewater Road.
Go past Unibuy department store (3) at the traffic lights and then cross the bridge over the canal.
On the corner on the left you can see Bloomingdale University (4) with its excellent library.
Turn right into Carnation Street. Go along here and and enjoy a nice view of the town lake from our Little Swan Lake café (5) on your right.
Our famous Holy Cross Cathedral (6) is nearby, on the corner of Carnation Street and Trinity Street.
Visit our old castle (7) up on the hill on the left. It's open for visitors every day, from 10 a.m. to 5 p.m., except Monday. Back in Rosehill Lane turn left and go along there.
In the first street on the left there's Bloomingdale's Museum of Gardening (8). The museum has an outdoor part, too!
For more information about Bloomingdale and its interesting history go to the Tourist Office (9) on the corner of Trinity Street and Station Road.
Your tour ends with a traditional meal at the oldest pub in town, the Red Lion (10), directly opposite the Tourist Office.

The *Real* Thing

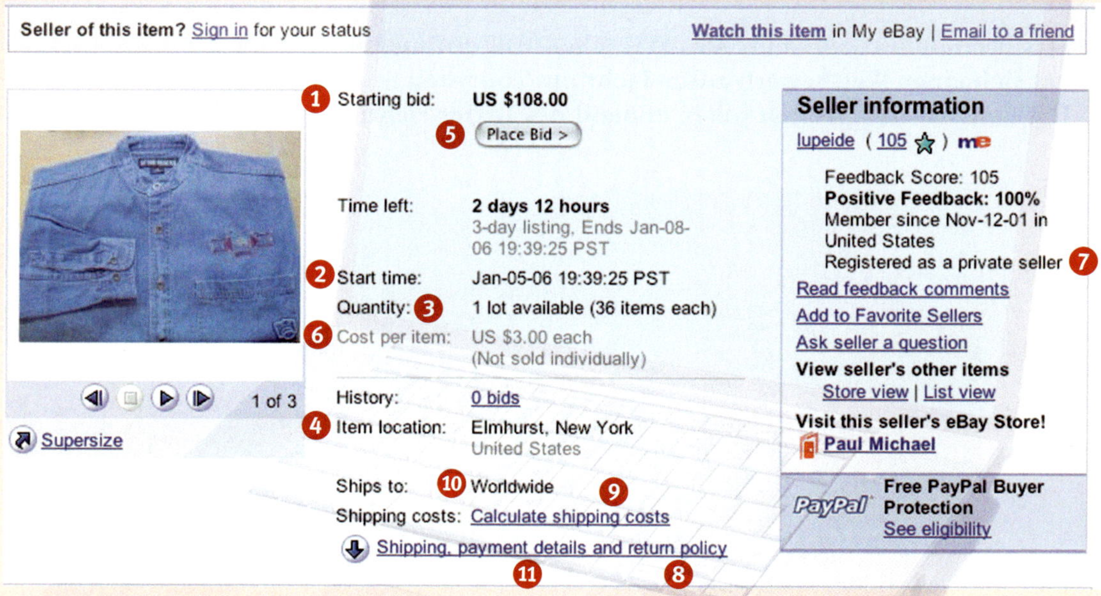

Ordnen Sie die folgenden Begriffe zu:

Anfangsgebot 1 privater Verkäufer ___ Angebotsbeginn ___ weltweit ___
Rücknahme(regelung) ___ Anzahl ___ Verandkosten ___ Artikelstandort ___
bieten ___ Zahlungsweise ___ Preis pro Stück ___

Online Shopping

You get anything on the internet. Really anything! There are a lot of advantages of shopping online: you can look for the lowest price and you have a wide range of options. You can visit a shop far away and order items that are not available in your area. Anything you buy will be delivered to your doorstep. Of course, you cannot touch the item, look at it, open it and take it home with you. But online shops offer something else: you see pictures, you can take a look at some pages, and you can read reviews by other customers who bought the same item.
You want to get an old toy you played with when you were a child? You want to sell old magazines nobody needs any more? Then auction websites, such as ebay® are a good place to go. You place a bid, and see if other people are also interested and the price gets higher. You can never be sure how much something will cost in the end. You have to decide how much you really want to spend.
And once you've had enough, you can simply sell the item again and may receive more than you paid – if you are lucky!

advantages: Vorteile; wide range of options: große Auswahl an Möglichkeiten; available: verfügbar; delivered: (to) deliver: liefern; doorstep: Haustür; (to) touch: berühren; reviews: Bewertungen, Besprechungen; toy: Spielzeug; auction: Auktion, Versteigerung; (to) place a bid: ein Gebot abgeben; simply: einfach; (to) receive: erhalten

My Portfolio

1 **Ergänzen Sie Ihr persönliches Vokabelheft mit folgenden Themen.**

Im Laden

I'm looking for an English dictionary. *Ich suche ein Englischwörterbuch.*

Wegbeschreibung

First, turn left at the church. *Zuerst biegen Sie links an der Kirche ab.*

Hilfe anbieten/annehmen

That's very kind of you. *Das ist sehr nett von Ihnen/dir.*

2 **Stellen Sie sich vor, ein englischer Kunde möchte Ihre Firma/Ihr Zuhause besuchen. Beschreiben Sie vom nächsten Bahnhof, der nächsten Bushaltestelle oder der nächsten U-Bahnhaltestelle den Weg auf Englisch wie er/sie zu Ihnen kommt.**

"When you leave the station turn left ..."

3 **Schließen Sie für einen Augenblick die Augen und denken Sie an einen schönen Urlaub zurück. Welche Dinge haben Sie dort alle eingekauft z.B. im Supermarkt, beim Bäcker, in der Apotheke, im Souvenirladen, auf der Post, im Hotel etc.? Notieren Sie diese, sodass Sie beim nächsten Mal gut vorbereitet sind und diese auf Englisch erfragen können. Nehmen Sie Ihr Wörterbuch zur Hilfe.**

In der Apotheke

Pflaster	*plaster*
Kopfschmerzen	*headache*
...	

Auf der Post

Briefmarke	*stamp*
...	

12 Looking back, looking ahead

Vocabulary & Phrases

1 **Ergänzen Sie die Ausdrücke aus dem Kasten.**

Welchen Beruf hat Jenny?

I have a *full-time* job, and I'm always ________ [1].
I have a full ________ [2] every day of the week.
My day ________ [3] at 6.45 most days,
and I ________ ________ [4] every evening.
I don't get any money for my work, but I don't pay ________ [5].
In my ________ [6] I have the times of swimming lessons,
birthday parties and things like that. My ________ [7] are six,
four, and two. They ________ [8] me busy round the clock.

begins • busy
clients • diary
~~full time~~
keep • schedule
tax • work late

2 **Bringen Sie je zwei Ausdrücke zusammen, die eine sinnvolle Wendung bilden.**

babysit	*in a neighbour's flat*	abroad
check your schedule		at the cinema
fly		at the gym
go on holiday		for the future
look for work		in a hot-air balloon
make plans		~~in a neighbour's flat~~
meet a client		in his or her office
relax		in the sauna
watch a film		in your diary
work out		in a newspaper

Grammar

3 **Vervollständigen Sie das Gespräch.**

MARK I thought we might go for a drink one evening next week. Are you free on Friday?

ALAN Sorry, *I'm going* (I / go) to a concert. _______________ [1] (you/do) anything on Thursday?

MARK Yes, I _______________ [2]. _______________ [3] (go swimming) with the children. _______________ [4] (you / work) at the weekend again?

ALAN (I / work) _______________ [5] on Sunday, but _______________ [6] (I / not work) on Saturday. Is Saturday OK for you?

MARK Sunday would be OK, but on Saturday I'm afraid _______________ [7] (our neighbours / have) a party, and we're invited.

ALAN What about the beginning of the week? What _______________ [8] (you / do) on Monday evening?

MARK _______________ [9] our other neighbours to the airport. That only leaves (I / take) Tuesday and Wednesday. You always go to your German class on Tuesday, right? _______________ [10] (you / go) next Tuesday?

ALAN No, _______________ [11]. But _______________ [12] (Alice & I / go) to the cinema. So that really only leaves Wednesday.

MARK It's OK for me. Is it OK for you?

ALAN Well, _______________ [13] (Alice / work) late, but if we say 9 o'clock, that would be OK.

MARK Nine o'clock it is!

Mixed Bag

4 **Beschreiben Sie, was Stella am heutigen Feiertag anders macht als üblicherweise.**

1 Stella usually ____________ at 6.30 a.m. But today is a holiday and she ____________ in bed.

2 It's 10 o'clock now and Stella ____________ in the park.
She normally ____________ a coffee break in her office at this time.

3 At 12.30 p.m. Stella always ____________ in the canteen. Today she ____________ in a café in town.

4 It's 3 o'clock and Stella ____________ her friend Margaret.
At this time Stella usually ____________ things with her boss.

5 At 5 o'clock Stella normally ____________ the office. Now she ____________ a book at home.

6 Stella usually ____________ to bed at 10.30 p.m. But today she ____________ a film at the cinema.

5 **Bilden Sie zu den Antworten passende Fragen.**

1 A (it / rain) *Is it raining?*
B No, the sun is out again.

2 A (do / you / what) ______________________________?
B I'm writing an email to Pete.

3 A (the soup / you / enjoy) ______________________________?
B Yes, it's delicious.

4 A (Jeff / again / work) ______________________________?
B No, he's still in hospital.

5 A (to bed / you / go) ______________________________?
B Yes, I'm very tired.

Remember **Die Verlaufsform der Gegenwart *(present continuous)***

I'm (not) work**ing**.	**Am** I work**ing**?	Yes, I **am**. No, **I'm not**.
You/We/They**'re (not)** work**ing**.	**Are** you/... work**ing**?	Yes, you/... **are**. No, you/...**'re not**. / No, you/... **aren't**.
He/She**'s (not)** work**ing**.	**Is** he/she work**ing**?	Yes, he/she **is**. No, he/she**'s not**. / No, he/she **isn't**.

6 A workaholic

English for eXperts

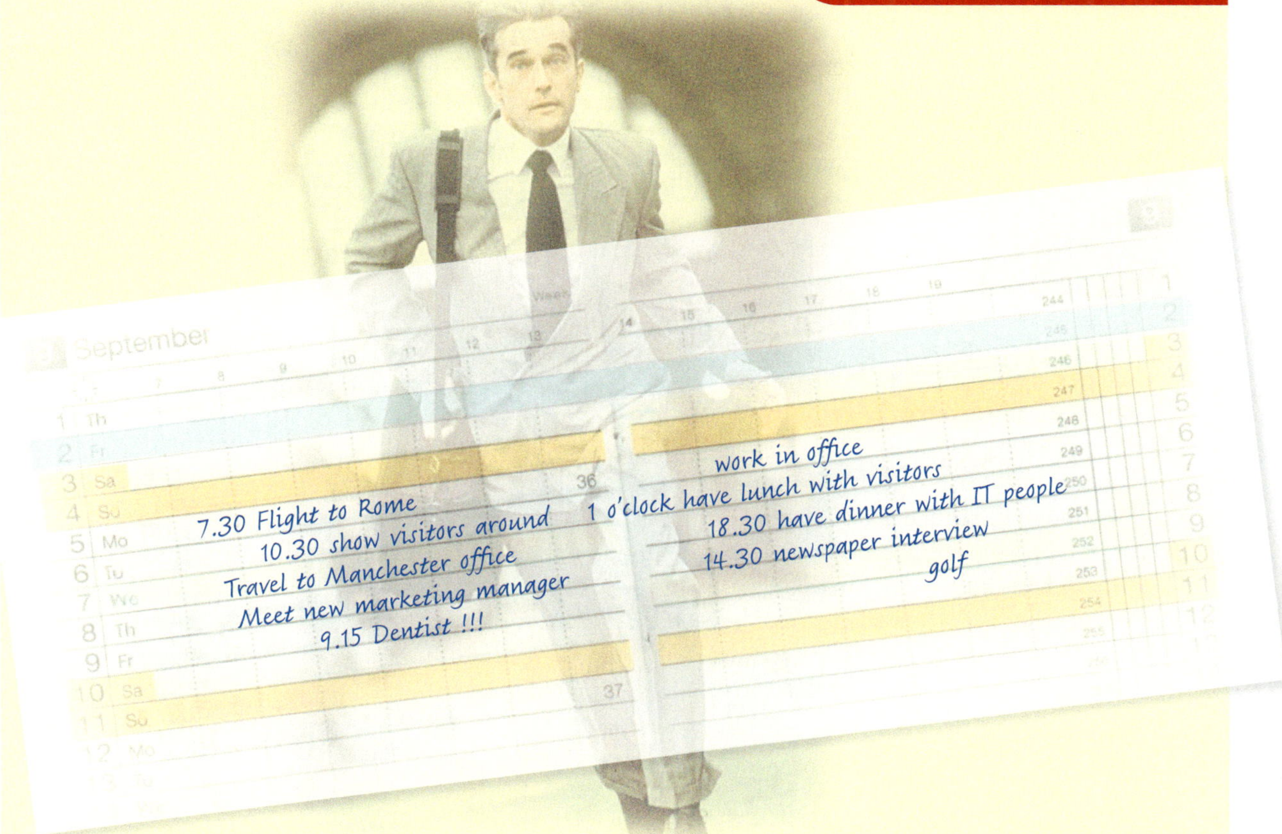

Ergänzen Sie den Text über Bill McCash anhand seines Terminkalenders.

Bill McCash is the owner of a big IT company in Edinburgh. Bill is a workaholic. His diary is always full. Next week is another very busy week for him.

On Monday *he's flying* to Rome to meet an important customer. He's ________[1] in the office again in the evening.

On Tuesday morning Bill ________[2] visitors around the company. After that ________[3] lunch with them.

On Wednesday ________[4] to his Manchester office. ________[5] a business dinner with some IT experts there in the evening.

The next day ________[6] the new marketing manager. In the afternoon ________[7] an interview with the local newspaper. On Friday morning ________[8] to the dentist and in the afternoon ________[9] golf.

The *Real* Thing

The end of London's moving landmark

The "Routemaster" (RM) is a model of red double-decker bus that was introduced in London in 1956. It stopped its regular service on 9 December 2005. Nearly 2,900 RMs were built. A standard model seats 64 passengers (28 downstairs and 36 upstairs). The RM was very popular with both Londoners and tourists because of the open platform at the back that gave passengers the freedom to hop on or off whenever they wanted to. They were designed for a 17-year life and the last RM started service in 1976. RMs were not fully accessible to wheelchair users or mothers with baby buggies, and were involved in more accidents than driver-only operated buses.

Every seat tells a story ...

Struggling to drive the bus

"I am not a great fan of the Routemasters. They are hard work. Everyone who drives a Routemaster earns their money. I remember the power steering was so bad you had to fight the bus all day and by the time I finished in the evening I felt like Arnie Schwarzenegger. My arms were enormous because I had been pushing and pulling all the time."

Daydreaming

"The thing which I like about travelling on buses, is the same thing I like about all forms of public transport: the chance to switch off. I can get on the bus, choose a seat, then sit and look out of the window while my mind wanders off. Time spent travelling is a "paused" time, in a "paused" place, the feeling of wasting time seldom comes across me. Daydreamers are more relaxed people."

A Conductor

"I often keep my eyes open and try to read passengers' body language to tell me who's getting off and who isn't. They might press the bell or they might not. So I often do that for them. Over the years you learn to recognize a confused person, can spot a person who is lost or who wants to go somewhere else but doesn't want to ask. You see all this and more!"

moving landmark: fahrbares Wahrzeichen; regular service: planmäßigen Betrieb; (to) hop on / hop off: ein und aussteigen; accessible: zugänglich; wheelchair users: Rollstuhlfahrer; involved: verwickelt (sein); struggling: kämpfen; power steering: Servolenkung; enormous: gewaltige; pushing and pulling: drücken und ziehen; (to) switch off: abschalten; mind: Gedanken; wanders off: (to) wander off: umherwandern; wasting time: Zeitverschwendung; bell: Klingel; (to) recognize: erkennen; confused: verwirrt; (to) spot: erkennen

My Portfolio

1 Wenn Sie nun zurückblicken, wie groß war Ihr Lernerfolg mit diesem Lehrwerk? Beantworten Sie folgende Fragen für sich selbst:

- Welche Situationen kann ich bereits auf Englisch meistern?
- Zu welchen Themen kann ich Fragen stellen und etwas erzählen?
- Welche neuen grammatischen Strukturen habe ich kennen gelernt?
- Wo habe ich noch Lücken?
- Was fällt mir besonders schwer? Woran könnte das liegen?

  Tipp: Sprechen Sie dies im nächsten Kurs bei Ihrer Kursleitung an.
- Habe ich alle die mir zur Verfügung stehenden Lernhilfen optimal genutzt wie z. B. *Phrasebook*, *Extra Language Trainer*, *Grammatikübersicht* und *Magazine* im Lehrwerk?
- Habe ich mir genügend Zeit zum Vor- und Nachbereiten genommen? Was könnte ich verbessern?
- Was möchte ich an meinem Lernverhalten ändern?
- Was sind meine Ziele für den Folgekurs?

2 Vervollständigen Sie Ihr persönliches *Sprachenportfolio* im Lehrwerk.

Insbesondere die *Checkliste zur Selbsteinschätzung* zeigt Ihnen noch einmal, was Sie bereits schon alles gelernt haben.

Ihr eigenes *Dossier* sollte alle zusätzliche Materialien enthalten, die Sie während des Kurses gesammelt haben, wobei diese in entsprechende Rubriken eingeordnet werden sollten (z. B. Grammatik, Lesetexte, Spiele, Wortschatz, Partnerübungen etc.), um eine bessere Übersicht zu bekommen.

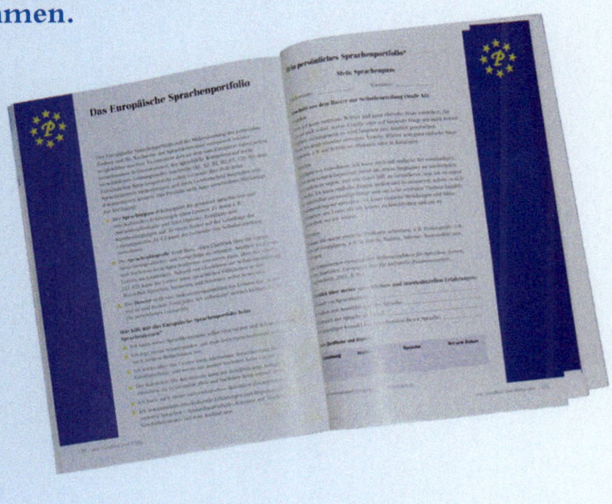

1 Family: *partner, mother, father*
Jobs: *computer programmer, journalist, teacher*
Transport: *bus, taxi, plane*
Food: *pizza, sandwich, spaghetti*

2 *make a phone call*
a flight ticket
my first name
an English teacher
a computer expert
a travel journalist

3
2 *on*
3 *at*
4 *to*

4
2 *Oh, sorry.*
3 *No problem.*
4 *Where are you from?*
5 *Nice to meet you.*
6 *What's the English for 'Ungarn'?*

5
2 *It's me.*
3 *I was born*
4 *I'm late*

6

Oldtimer	veteran car
City	city centre
Smoking	dinner jacket
Beamer	(video) projector
Kartoffelchips	potato crisps
Pommes Frites	chips
(Park-)Bank	bench

The Real Thing

1 1 + 3
2 + 8
5 + 7
2 4: SPEED LIMIT 45 = Angabe der Geschwindigkeitsbegrenzung (45 mph); 6: FALLING ROCK = Steinschlag

My Portfolio

1 S. 4–5, *Table of contents*
2 *Magazine* für das Selbststudium, Lerntipps, Hinweise zum Sprachenportfolio
3 FCA1 S. 130–135 und FCA1 Fast S. 90–94
4 FCA1 S. 159 und FCA1 Fast S. 129
5 FCA1 S. 138–139 und FCA1 Fast S.105
6 *Magazine & Quick Check*, FCA1 S. 153-158 und FCA1 Fast S. 120–124
7 S. 82–93
8 FCA1 S. 80–81 und FCA1 Fast S. 76–77
9 FCA1 S.146–152 und FCA1 Fast S. 113–119
10 Mit dieser Lücke können die neuen Wörter besser gelernt werden, da nur das deutsche Wort sichtbar ist, nicht aber das englische, dessen Lautschrift sowie der englische Beispielsatz.
11 Begriffe, die im Amerikanischen (AE) eine abweichende Aussprache haben, sind mit ‚AE' gekennzeichnet.

Vocabulary & Phrases

1

2 *phone number*
3 *text message*
4 *credit card*
5 *email address*

7 *email address*
8 *text message*
9 *credit card*
10 *phone number*

2

evening and *day*
room and *hotel*
letter and *word*
page and *book*

2 *letter, word*
3 *room, hotel*
4 *page, book*
5 *day, evening*

3

1 Can I have your name, please?
2 Yes, it's Gaunt.

3 Sorry, what was that again?
4 Gaunt.
5 Oh, can you spell that for me, please?
6 G – A – U – N-T.
7 Ah, Gaunt. And what's your first name, Mr Gaunt?
8 Harry.
9 And what's your phone number, please?
10 020-7273621.
11 020-7273621. OK, I've got that. And your mobile number?
12 Sorry, I don't have a mobile.

4

fifty-five pounds fifteen
fourteen pounds forty-four

5

oh six oh two, nine one five four double seven

6

32	*23*	*twenty-three*
13	*31*	*thirty-one*
45	*54*	*fifty-four*
78	*87*	*eighty-seven*
94	*49*	*forty-nine*

7

2 a
3 f
4 c
b und d passen nicht.

8

1 d
2 c
3 b
4 a

The *Real* Thing

bis zu	*Up to*
Geschlecht	*Sex*
Familienstand	*Marital status*
verheiratet	*Married*
verlobt	*Engaged*
getrennt	*Separated*
geschieden	*Divorced*
verwitwet	*Widowed*
unverheiratet	*Never married*
Geburtsort	*Place of birth*

Vocabulary & Phrases

1 2 f 3 d 4 e 5 b 6 a

2
2 … a glass **of** water, please?
3 … **on** the phone in his office.
4 … works **for** a bank.
5 … a member **of** your family?
6 … a photo **of** my brother and his family.

3 *article & magazine, daughter & son, good & bad, big & little, boss & colleague, sing & song*

Grammar

4
2 *Who*
3 *Who*
4 *Where*
5 *Where*
6 *Who*

5
2 *what*
3 *Who*
4 *Where*

6
2 *They*
3 *She*
4 *They*
5 *We*
6 *you*

7 Ben's not in his office. He's in the café. It's Serena's café. Ben's boss, Mrs Morgan, is on the phone. She's in Ben's office. Winston's in the office, too. He's Ben's colleague.

8
1 *are*
2 *We're*
3 *our*
4 *It's*
5 *His*
6 *They're*
7 *Their*
8 *Her*
9 *She's*

9
2 *Yes, he is.*
3 *No, he's not. / No, he isn't. (He's a magazine journalist.)*
4 *Yes, she is.*
5 *Yes, she is.*
6 *No, he's not. / No, he isn't. (He's William's brother.)*

8 *Is he (Richard) a journalist?*
9 *Is Eliza a tennis player?*
10 *Is Martin Eliza's son?*
11 *Is Eliza a pilot?*
12 *Is Eliza married?*

10
1 She *works* for easyJet. She *plays* volleyball, and she *has* two children.

2 *Barbara lives in Scotland. She is a/works as a teacher. She plays the piano, and she has two children.*
3 *Richard lives in Manchester. He is a/works as a magazine journalist. He plays tennis, and he has two children.*

Mixed Bag

11 *4 6 3 5* 2 *7 8* 1

12
Ian + Evelyn
Christine + Wayne *Michael + Angela*
John *Tom* *Peter* *Emma*

13
2 *Frank Baker*
3 *Bath, England*
4 *Diana Morrow*
5 *New Zealand*
6 *Jennifer Hornby*

14 2 false 3 false 4 false 5 true 6 false

The Real Thing

Sein Talent als Discjockey.

Vocabulary & Phrases

1 *Pizza* margherita (*cheese* and *tomato*)
Hamburger and *chips*
Vegetable curry
Chicken nuggets
Or try one of our *sandwiches* or help yourself from the *salad* bar.
Chocolate mousse
Fruit salad
Tea and *coffee*
Mineral water

2
2 *by*
3 *at, on*
4 *about*
5 *round*
6 *out, for*

3 I love, I like, I quite like, I don't like, I hate

Grammar

4
3 *I like* curry.
4 *I like* Beethoven.
5 *I don't like* warm beer.
6 *I don't like* hamburgers.
7 *I like* Riesling.
8 *I don't like* mobile phones.

1 *likes*
2 *doesn't like*
3 *likes*
4 *likes*
5 *likes*
6 *doesn't like*

5
1 *have*
2 *comes*
3 *work*
4 *don't have*
5 *doesn't have*
6 *like*
7 *speaks*
8 *doesn't speak*
9 *speaks*
10 *don't speak*

6
1 *do you like it*
2 *do you have*
3 do *they speak*
4 *do you live*
5 *Do you like it*

Mixed Bag

7
1 *Oh yes, I do!*
2 *No, I don't.*

8
1 *of*
2 *do*
3 *would*
4 *much*
5 *thanks*
6 *please*
7 *Here*
8 *rice*
9 *There's*
10 *Asian*
11 *sushi*

The *Real* Thing

1 At 'The Bear'. / You can eat traditional food at "The Bear".
2 At 'The Bear'. / You can have a vegetarian meal at "The Bear".
3 At 'The Bear' and 'The White Horse'. / You can have lunch at "The Bear" and "The White Horse".
4 'The White Horse'. / "The White Horse" and "The Bear" serve coffee.

Vocabulary & Phrases

1

2 have breakfast on the way to work
3 drink coffee in the morning break
4 have lunch in the canteen
5 take an afternoon nap
6 start work again
7 have the evening meal
8 watch TV till midnight
9 go to bed
10 sleep till morning

2 ten to two
3 ten past two
4 twenty past two
5 half past two
6 twenty to three
7 quarter to three
8 quarter past three
9 half past three

2

2 *have, shower*
3 *start*
4 *eat, main*
5 *watch*
6 *go to*

Grammar

3

2 When *do you start work*?
3 Where *do you work*?
4 When *do you have lunch*?
5 Do *you work at* the weekend?
6 *Do you like* your boss?

4

2 *She gets up*
She doesn't get up
3 *She watches*
She doesn't watch
4 *She doesn't eat her main meal*
She eats her main meal
5 *She starts work*
She doesn't start work

I think she's *a system administrator.*

Mixed Bag

5

1 at
2 before
3 between
4 past
5 from
6 for
7 after

6

2 *It's twenty to five.*
3 *It's quarter past seven.*
4 *It's quarter past ten (in the evening).*
5 *It's five to twelve.*
6 *It's half past one.*
7 *It's half past two (in the afternoon).*
8 *It's quarter to ten.*

7

1 *makes*
2 *likes*
3 *goes*
4 *open*
5 *walks*
6 *doesn't go*
7 *has*
8 *doesn't go*
9 *sees*
10 *doesn't meet*
11 *meets*
12 *goes*
13 *works*

8

A Excuse me, *can you tell me the time, please?*
B *It's quarter past two.*
A Thanks.

The *Real* Thing

1 False
2 True
3 False
4 False
5 False
6 True

Vocabulary & Phrases

1
6 *SATURDAY*
7 *SUNDAY*
2 *TUESDAY*
1 MONDAY
4 *THURSDAY*
3 *WEDNESDAY*
5 *FRIDAY*

2
2 *Perhaps*
3 *actually*
4 *everything*
5 *never*
6 *true*
7 *definitely*

Grammar

3 Example:
I *always/usually/often/sometimes/never* go out on Sunday evening …

4
2 We don't *usually* cook lunch on Sunday. We *usually* have brunch.
3 I am *usually* at home at the weekend. But I *sometimes* go to the office.
4 I *never* have lunch in the canteen. I *usually* have only a snack.
5 My partner is *often* up before me on Sunday morning. I *usually* get up quite late.
6 Do you *always* go shopping on Thursday evening? Is that *always* your shopping evening?

5 2 d 3 a 4 e 5 c

6
2 *I get up early every day.*
3 *I leave home at 7.15.*
4 *I'm in the office before 8 o'clock.*
5 *People at my office have lunch between 12.30 and 1.00.*
6 *I often go shopping.*

Mixed Bag

7
2 *for*
3 *in*
4 *to*
5 *about*
6 *on*

8

am Montag	*on Monday*
zu Hause	*at home*
bei der Arbeit	*at work*
am Geburtstag	*on (my) birthday*
auf Englisch	*in English*
in Deutschland	*in Germany*
am Wochenende	*at the weekend*
in einer Besprechung	*in a meeting*
am Telefon	*on the (tele)phone*
im Urlaub	*on holiday*
am Abend	*in the evening*

9 Dave, Mike and Tina always meet in a pub on *Tuesday evening.*

The *Real* Thing

2

Filmgestalten	characters
Dokumentarfilm	documentary
Fernsehsender	TV channel
Komödie	comedy
Lotterie	lottery
Presseüberblick	press review
Quizsendung	quiz show
Schauspieler, Darsteller	actors
Spielfilm	feature film

3

Outstanding	*hervorragend*
Very good	*sehr gut*
Worth watching	*sehenswert*
Could be worse	*nicht ganz schlecht*
Poor	*schwach*

Vocabulary & Phrases

1
1 *MOTORBIKE*
2 *BIKE*
3 *BUS*
4 *CAR*
5 *TAXI*
6 *PLANE*
7 *TRAIN*
8 *UNDERGROUND*

The highlighted word is: *TRAVEL*.

2
35 minutes ago
an hour ago
last *Sunday*
two weeks ago
last *September*

3
1 *four days ago*
2 *three days ago*
3 *an hour ago*
4 *ten minutes ago*

4
2 *have a holiday*
3 *have a meeting*
4 *have a party*
5 *have a date*
6 *have a shower / wash*
7 *have a drink*
8 *have a rest / break*

Grammar

5
2 *answered*
3 *finished*
4 *hated*
5 *said*
6 *talked*
7 *watched*
8 *thought*
9 *went*
10 *drank*
11 *wrote*
12 *found*

6
2 *I didn't know*
3 *I didn't see*
4 *I didn't know*
5 *I didn't want*
6 *I didn't have / know*
7 *you didn't ask*

7
2 Why *did you get* home so late?
3 Why *did you go* into town?
4 Where *did you have* this appointment?
5 Who *did you* meet?
6 What *did you talk* about?

Mixed Bag

8
1 *was*
2 *was*
3 *didn't go*
4 *didn't have*
5 *walked*
6 *went*
7 *played*
8 *didn't have*
9 *was*
10 *was*
11 *didn't have*
12 *visited*
13 *was*
14 *were*
15 *had*
16 *didn't need*
17 *had*
18 *saw*
19 *didn't speak*
20 *knew*
21 *had*
22 *told*
23 *was*
24 *asked*
25 *went*

9
... did you go to the shops?
What did you buy?
What did you do then?
What did you do there?
How long did you sleep?
What did you do then?

The Real Thing

1 £8 on weekdays.
2 No, you don't.
3 It's free at the weekend.
4 At pay points or at petrol stations and shops.
5 By public transport.

Vocabulary & Phrases

1

2 Christmas is *on (the) 25th of December* and people say *Happy Christmas* or *Merry Christmas*.
3 New Year's day is *on (the) 1st of January* and people say *Happy New Year*.
4 My birthday is *on (the) ...* and people say *Happy Birthday*.

2

2 *go sightseeing*
3 *go walking*
4 *go on holiday / go away*
5 *go swimming*
6 *go skiing*

9 f 10 a 11 d 12 c 13 b 14 e

Grammar

3

1 *gave*
2 *was*
3 *thought*
4 *was*
5 *organized*
6 *didn't cook*
7 *planned*
8 *bought*
9 *wrote*
10 *wasn't*
11 *sent*
12 *got*
13 *went*
14 *spent*
15 *sat*
16 *did*
17 *came*
18 *was*
19 *were*
20 *had*
21 *was*
22 *didn't rain*
23 *had*

4

1 *Where did you stay?*
2 *What did you pay?*
3 *Did you have a good time?*
4 *Why was that?*
5 *So what did you do?*
6 *Were you away long?*

Mixed Bag

5

thirty-one days:	thirty days:
January	
March	*April*
May	*June*
July	
August	*September*
October	*November*
December	

February

6

1 *between*
2 *at*
3 *after*
4 *in*
5 *on*
6 *from*
7 *for*

7

2 *third-rate*
3 *second language*
4 *first aid*
5 *first-class hotel*
6 *second hand*

The *Real* Thing

1 Foinhaven, Stromness, Mrs Wishart
2 Kirkwall, Orkney, Mrs J Hume
3 Shoreside, South Ronaldsay, Tracey Jackson
4 Stenness, Orkney, Mrs M C R Page

Vocabulary & Phrases

1

2 *playground*
3 *lake*
4 *airport*
5 *bridge*
6 *hills/mountains*
7 *station*
8 *museum*
9 *cinema*
10 *church*

There are also a lot other details: boat, bus, plane, houses, cars, traffic lights, island, dog …

2

2 *high/tall*
3 *southeast*
4 *dry*
5 *worst*

7 *large*
8 *well-known*
9 *relatives/relations*
10 *home*

3

1 *was born*
2 *grew up*
3 *met*
4 *lives*
5 *got married*
6 *retired*
7 *died*
8 *stay*

Grammar

4

1 *sunnier*
2 *hottest*
3 *worse*
4 *wetter*
5 *cooler*
6 *cheaper*
7 *more expensive*
8 *larger*
9 *smaller*
10 *most famous*
11 *than*
12 *than*
13 *as*

5

1 *there are*
2 *There aren't*
3 *is there*
4 *Is there*
5 *there's*
6 *there isn't*
7 *there isn't*
8 *Are there*
9 *There are*

10 *any*
11 *some*
12 *any*
13 *some*
14 *any*

Mixed Bag

6

2 *museum*
3 *river*
4 *festival*
5 *bridge*
6 *cathedral*
7 *desert*
8 *university*

10 *longest*
11 *most expensive*
12 *busiest*
13 *most famous*
14 *driest*
15 *most beautiful*

7

Name	Marc	*Pete*	*Rhonda*	*Claire*
Job	*politician*	*singer*	*model*	*teacher*
Age	*43*	*36*	*34*	*30*

8

2 *write, right*
3 *a round, around*
4 *buy, bye*
5 *know, No*
6 *hour, our*
7 *see, sea*
8 *son, sun*
9 *to, Two*

Vocabulary & Phrases

1
1 *orange orange*
2 *black remote control*
3 *brown coffee (beans)*
4 *yellow banana*
5 *green grass*
6 *white snow*
7 *red traffic light*

2
2 *ear, hear*
3 *fingers, feel*
4 *nose, smell*
5 *tongue, taste*

6 *smells*
7 *hear*
8 *see*
9 *feel*

3
1 *Just a moment, please.*
2 *I'm afraid Ms Koch is not here.*
3 *Would you like to leave a message?*
4 *Can I take a message?*
5 *I'm sorry, there was a problem with the line.*
6 *OK. I'll tell Hannah (that) you called.*

Grammar

4
2 *doing*
3 *listening*
4 *watching*
5 *doing*

5
2 *busy*
3 *organized*
4 *musical*
5 *serious*
6 *athletic*
7 *quiet*

Mixed Bag

6
2 *comedies*
3 *being with lots of people*
4 *working in a team*
5 *doing sports*
6 *listening to loud music*
7 *dancing*
8 *dynamic*
9 *walking in the rain*

10 *rainy weather*
11 *sitting at home*
12 *reading*
13 *listening to music*
14 *sport*
15 *surfing the internet*
16 *going shopping*
17 *being her own boss*

7
1 I'll give Ms Johnson your message.
2 Can I speak to Danny, please?
3 Do you want to leave a message?
4 How can I help you?
5 I'm afraid Danny is still at school.
6 I'll call again later.
7 I'd like to speak to your sales manager, please.
8 Can you ask her to call back before lunch?

The *Real* Thing

1 The teacher and the man from Islington

Call Voicebox
●Teacher, 53, enjoys swimming & reading, music looking to meet M, 45 & 65 to see what happens... Herts. Call Voicebox
walk...
intellig...
Voicebox

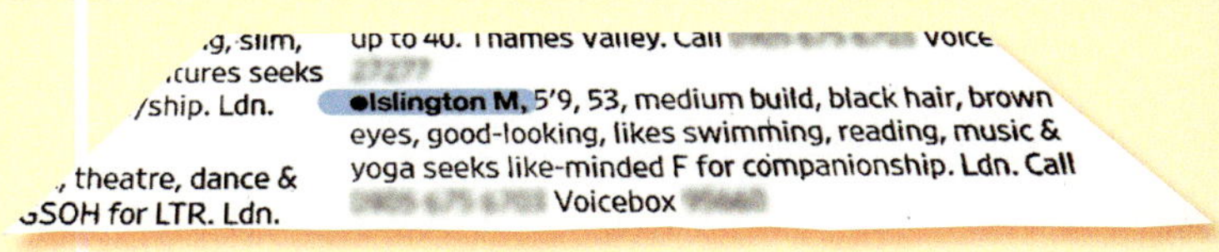
..g, slim,
..tures seeks
/ship. Ldn.
, theatre, dance &
GSOH for LTR. Ldn.
up to 40. Thames Valley. Call Voice
●Islington M, 5'9, 53, medium build, black hair, brown eyes, good-looking, likes swimming, reading, music & yoga seeks like-minded F for companionship. Ldn. Call Voicebox

Vocabulary & Phrases

1
2 *brush*
3 *hairdryer*
4 *hat(s)*
5 *walking boots*
6 *sunglasses*
7 *comb(s)*
8 *sunscreen*

2
2 *suitcase*
3 *guidebook*
4 *phrasebook*
5 *valuables*
6 *petrol station*

3
1 *like*
2 *love*
3 *would*
4 *could*

4 *Alternative 1:*
Well, you go along here, straight on along Blackwell Road. Turn right into Crendon Street and go along there past the Watersmith Bookshop. The shopping centre is opposite the bookshop, on the right, on the corner of New Street and Crendon Street.
Alternative 2:
Well, you go along here, then turn right into Eastern Street. Go along there, and turn left into New Street. The shopping centre is at the end of New Street, on the corner of New Street and Crendon Street, opposite the bookshop.

Grammar

5
2 *I'll see*
3 *I'll help*
4 *I'll wait*
5 *I'll give*
6 *I'll take*

Mixed Bag

6 A–Z Directory:
9 *Bookshop*
13 *Drugstore*
1 Entrance
2 Information
4 Lifts
7 *Luggage*
11 *Shoes*
10 *Sports equipment*
3 Stairs
6 Telephone
5 Toilets
8 *Toys & Games*
12 Young fashion

7

The *Real* Thing

1	Anfangsgebot	starting bid
2	Angebotsbeginn	start time
3	Anzahl	quantity
4	Artikelstandort	item location
5	Bieten	place (a) bid
6	Preis pro Stück	cost per item
7	privater Verkäufer	private seller
8	Rücknahme(regelung)	return policy
9	Verandkosten	shipping costs
10	weltweit	worldwide
11	Zahlungsweise	payment details

Vocabulary & Phrases

1
1 *busy*
2 *schedule*
3 *begins*
4 *work late*
5 *tax*
6 *diary*
7 *clients*
8 *keep*

2
check your schedule *in your diary*
fly *in a hot-air balloon*
go on holiday *abroad*
look for work *in a newspaper*
make plans *for the future*
meet a client *in his or her office*
relax *in the sauna*
watch a film *at the cinema*
work out *at the gym*

Grammar

3
1 *Are you doing*
2 *am*
3 *I'm going swimming*
4 *Are you working*
5 *I'm working*
6 *I'm not working*
7 *our neighbours are having*
8 *are you doing*
9 *I'm taking*
10 *Are you going*
11 *I'm not*
12 *Alice & I are going*
13 *Alice is working*

Mixed Bag

4
1 *gets up, is lying*
2 *is jogging, has*
3 *eats (lunch), is sitting / is eating*
4 *is visiting, discusses*
5 *leaves, is reading*
6 *goes, is watching*

5
2 *What are you doing?*
3 *Are you enjoying the soup?*
4 *Is Jeff working again?*
5 *Are you going to bed?*

6
1 *working*
2 *is showing*
3 *he's having*
4 *he's travelling*
5 *He's having*
6 *he's meeting*
7 *he's having*
8 *he's going*
9 *he's playing*

A, a

a lot of [ə 'lɒt əv] *viel, viele*
a.m. [ˌeɪ 'em] *von Mitternacht bis Mittag*
about [ə'baʊt] *über; etwa, ungefähr*
abroad [ə'brɔːd] *im Ausland*
accessible [ək'sesəbl] *zugänglich*
accident ['æksɪdənt] *Unfall*
accommodation [əˌkɒmə'deɪʃn] *Unterkunft, Zimmer*
(to) **act** [ækt] *schauspielern*
action film ['ækʃn fɪlm] *Actionfilm*
activity [æk'tɪvəti] *Aktivität, Beschäftigung, Tätigkeit*
actor ['æktə] *Schauspieler*
actually ['æktʃuəli] *eigentlich, wirklich, tatsächlich*
address [ə'dres] *Adresse*
(to) **admire** [əd'maɪə] *bewundern*
advantage [əd'vɑːntɪdʒ] *Vorteil, Vorzug*
afraid: I'm afraid [aɪm ə'freɪd] *leider*
after ['ɑːftə] *nach, nachdem*
afternoon [ˌɑːftə'nuːn] *Nachmittag*
afterwards ['ɑːftəwədz] *nachher, danach, hinterher*
again [ə'gen] *wieder, noch einmal*
age [eɪdʒ] *Alter*
ago [ə'gəʊ] *vor*
ahead [ə'hed] *(nach) vorne, voraus*
airport ['eəpɔːt] *Flughafen*
ale [eɪl] *Ale*
all [ɔːl] *alle, alles*
allergic [ə'lɜːdʒɪk] *allergisch*
alone [ə'ləʊn] *allein(e)*
along [ə'lɒŋ] *entlang*
already [ɔːl'redi] *schon, bereits*
also ['ɔːlsəʊ] *auch, außerdem*
always ['ɔːlweɪz] *immer*
and [ənd] *und*
angry ['æŋgri] *zornig, wütend*
another [ə'nʌðə] *noch eine/r/s, ein/e weitere/r/s*
(to) **answer** ['ɑːnsə] *beantworten, antworten*
answering machine ['ɑːnsərɪŋ məʃiːn] *Anrufbeantworter*
any ['eni] *irgendetwas, -welche*
  anything ['eniθɪŋ] *etwas, alles*
application [ˌæplɪ'keɪʃn] *Antrag, Bewerbung*
appointment [ə'pɔɪntmənt] *Termin, Verabredung*
area ['eəriə] *Gebiet, Gegend*
  residential area [reziˌdenʃl 'eəriə] *Wohngebiet*
arm [ɑːm] *Arm*
around: (to) **show sb around** [ˌʃəʊ ə'raʊnd] *jdn herumführen*
arrest [ə'rest] *Verhaftung, Festnahme*
(to) **arrive** [ə'raɪv] *ankommen, eintreffen*
article ['ɑːtɪkl] *Artikel*
as [əz] *als*
  as … as [əz əz] *(genau)so … wie*
  as well as [əz 'wel əz] *sowohl … als auch, sowie, neben*
(to) **ask** [ɑːsk] *fragen, bitten, einladen*
assistant [ə'sɪstənt] *Verkäufer/in*
at [ət, æt] *in, an, bei, auf*
  at home [ət 'həʊm] *zu Hause*
  at … o'clock [ət ə'klɒk] *um … Uhr*
  at work [ət 'wɜːk] *bei der Arbeit*
athletic [æθ'letɪk] *sportlich*
auction ['ɔːkʃn] *Versteigerung, Auktion*
aunt [ɑːnt] *Tante*
available [ə'veɪləbl] *verfügbar*
away [ə'weɪ] *weg, entfernt*

B, b

baby ['beɪbi] *Baby, Säugling, Kind*
  baby buggy ['beɪbi bʌgi] *Kinderwagen*
  baby daughter ['beɪbi dɔːtə] *Tochter, „Töchterchen"*
(to) **babysit** ['beɪbisɪt] *babysitten*
back [bæk] *zurück; Rückseite, hinterer Teil*
background ['bækgraʊnd] *Hintergrund, Herkunft*
backpack ['bækpæk] *Rucksack*
bad [bæd] *schlecht, nicht gut, schlimm*
bag [bæg] *Tasche, Tüte, Reisetasche*
balloon [bə'luːn] *Ballon*
bank [bæŋk] *Bank*
bar [bɑː] *Bar*
barbecue ['bɑːbɪkjuː] *Grill, Grillparty*
barbell ['bɑːbel] *Hantel*
bathroom ['bɑːθruːm] *Bad(ezimmer)*
(to) **be** [bi] *sein*
  (to) **be late** [bi 'leɪt] *zu spät kommen, spät (dran) sein, sich verspäten*
  (to) **be lost** [bi 'lɒst] *sich verlaufen haben*
  (to) **be lucky** [bi 'lʌki] *Glück haben*
  (to) **be sorry** [bi 'sɒri] *Leid tun*
beach [biːtʃ] *Strand*
bear [beə] *Bär*
beautiful ['bjuːtɪfl] *schön*
because [bɪ'kɒz] *weil*
(to) **become** [bɪ'kʌm] *werden*
bed [bed] *Bett*
bed and breakfast [ˌbed ən 'brekfəst] *Frühstückspension*
beer [bɪə] *Bier*
before [bɪ'fɔː] *vor, vorher, zuvor, bevor*
beginning [bɪ'gɪnɪŋ] *Anfang, Beginn*
(to) **believe (in)** [bɪ'liːv ɪn] *glauben (an)*
bell [bel] *Klingel, Glocke*
bench [bentʃ] *Bank, Sitzbank*
best [best] *beste/r/s*
better ['betə] *besser*
between [bɪ'twiːn] *zwischen*
(to) **bid** [bɪd] *bieten*
big [bɪg] *groß*
bike [baɪk] *Fahrrad, Rad*
billion ['bɪljən] *Milliarde*
billionaire [ˌbɪljə'neə] *Milliardär/in*
biography [baɪ'ɒgrəfi] *Biographie*
birthday ['bɜːθdeɪ] *Geburtstag*
bit: a bit [ə 'bɪt] *ein bisschen, etwas*
bitter ['bɪtə] *halbdunkles, obergäriges Bier; bitter*
body ['bɒdi] *Körper*
  bodybuilding ['bɒdibɪldɪŋ] *Bodybuilding*
  bodybuilder ['bɒdibɪldə] *Bodybuilder*
book [bʊk] *Buch*
  (to) **book** [bʊk] *buchen, reservieren*
  bookshop ['bʊkʃɒp] *Buchhandlung*
born: (to) **be born** [bi 'bɔːn] *geboren werden/sein*
boss [bɒs] *Chef/in*
both: both … and [bəʊθ ənd] *beide, sowohl … als auch*
bottle ['bɒtl] *Flasche*
box [bɒks] *Kasten, Kästchen*
boy [bɔɪ] *Junge*
boyfriend ['bɔɪfrend] *Freund*
bread [bred] *Brot*
break [breɪk] *Pause*
breakfast ['brekfəst] *Frühstück*
bridge [brɪdʒ] *Brücke*
brother ['brʌðə] *Bruder*
brunch [brʌntʃ] *Brunch*
brush [brʌʃ] *Bürste*

buggy ['bʌgi] *Kinderwagen*
(to) **build** [bɪld] *bauen*
building ['bɪldɪŋ] *Gebäude*
bus [bʌs] *(Linien-)Bus*
business ['bɪznəs] *Firma, Geschäft(e), Unternehmen*
busy ['bɪzi] *beschäftigt, arbeitsreich, hektisch*
but [bʌt] *aber*
button ['bʌtn] *Taste, Knopf*
(to) **buy** [baɪ] *kaufen*
by [baɪ] *um, an, neben*
by car [baɪ 'kɑ:] *mit dem Auto*
by the way [baɪ ðə 'weɪ] *übrigens, nebenbei*

C, c

call [kɔ:l] *Anruf, Telefongespräch*
call centre ['kɔ:l sentə] *Callcenter*
(to) **call** [kɔ:l] *anrufen, rufen*
called [kɔ:ld] *namens, genannt*
can [kæn] *dürfen, können*
canal [kə'næl] *Kanal*
canteen [kæn'ti:n] *Kantine*
capital ['kæpɪtl] *Hauptstadt*
car [kɑ:] *Auto*
card [kɑ:d] *Karte*
career [kə'rɪə] *Werdegang, Karriere, Laufbahn*
carnation [kɑ:'neɪʃn] *Nelke*
carrot ['kærət] *Karotte, Möhre*
(to) **carry** ['kæri] *tragen, befördern*
castle ['kɑ:sl] *Burg, Schloss*
cat [kæt] *Katze*
catering ['keɪtərɪŋ] *Versorgung mit Speisen und Getränken*
cathedral [kə'θi:drəl] *Dom, Kathedrale*
cello ['tʃeləʊ] *Cello*
central ['sentrəl] *zentral, Zentral-*
centre ['sentə] *Zentrum*
certainly ['sɜ:tnli] *sicherlich, gewiss, natürlich*
chairman ['tʃeəmən] *Vorsitzender*
championship ['tʃæmpiənʃɪp] *Meisterschaft*
chance [tʃɑ:ns] *Gelegenheit, Möglichkeit*
channel ['tʃænl] *Kanal, Sender*
character ['kærəktə] *(Roman-/Film-)Figur, Person*
characteristics [ˌkærəktə'rɪstɪks] *typische Merkmale, Eigenschaften*
cheap [tʃi:p] *billig, günstig*
(to) **check** [tʃek] *(über)prüfen, kontrollieren*
cheers [tʃɪəz] *Prosit*
cheese [tʃi:z] *Käse*
chicken ['tʃɪkɪn] *Huhn, Hähnchen*
child, children [tʃaɪld, 'tʃɪldrən] *Kind, Kinder*
chips [tʃɪps] *Pommes frites*
chocolate ['tʃɒklət] *Schokolade, Praline*
choice [tʃɔɪs] *Wahl*
(to) **choose** [tʃu:z] *(aus)wählen, (sich) aussuchen*
church [tʃɜ:tʃ] *Kirche*
cinema ['sɪnəmə] *Kino*
citizen ['sɪtɪzn] *(Staats-)Bürger/in*
city ['sɪti] *(Groß-, Innen-)Stadt*
city centre [ˌsɪti 'sentə] *(Stadt-)Zentrum*
class [klɑ:s] *(Schul-)Klasse, Unterricht(sstunde), Kurs*
classical ['klæsɪkl] *klassisch*
(to) **clean** [kli:n] *putzen, reinigen, sauber machen, säubern*
client ['klaɪənt] *Kunde/Kundin*
clock [klɒk] *Uhr*
close [kləʊs] *nahe*
clothes [kləʊðz] *Kleidung, Kleider*
club [klʌb] *Klub*
clue [klu:] *Hinweis, Tipp*
coffee ['kɒfi] *Kaffee*
cold [kəʊld] *kalt*
colleague ['kɒli:g] *Kollege/Kollegin*
comb [kəʊm] *Kamm*
(to) **come** [kʌm] *kommen*
(to) **come across** [ˌkʌm ə'krɒs] *begegnen*
comedy ['kɒmədi] *Komödie*
common: in common [ɪn 'kɒmən] *gemeinsam*
commuter [kə'mju:tə] *Pendler/in*
company ['kʌmpəni] *Unternehmen, Firma, Gesellschaft*
computer [kəm'pju:tə] *Computer*
concert ['kɒnsət] *Konzert*
conductor [kən'dʌktə] *Schaffner/in*
conflict ['kɒnflɪkt] *Konflikt*
confused [kən'fju:zd] *verwirrt*
contact ['kɒntækt] *Kontakt, Verbindung*
(to) **contact** ['kɒntækt] *sich in Verbindung setzen mit, sich wenden an*
controversial [ˌkɒntrə'vɜ:ʃl] *kontrovers, umstritten*
conversation [ˌkɒnvə'seɪʃn] *Gespräch, Unterhaltung*
(to) **cook** [kʊk] *zubereiten, machen, kochen*
cool [ku:l] *kühl*
corner ['kɔ:nə] *Ecke*
(to) **cost** [kɒst] *kosten*
could [kʊd] *könnte/n*
council ['kaʊnsl] *Rat*
country ['kʌntri] *Land, Staat*
countryside ['kʌntrisaɪd] *Landschaft*
course: of course [əf 'kɔ:s] *natürlich, selbstverständlich*
creative [kri'eɪtɪv] *kreativ, schöpferisch*
credit card ['kredɪt kɑ:d] *Kreditkarte*
crisps [krɪsps] *Kartoffelchips*
cross [krɒs] *Kreuz*
(to) **cross** [krɒs] *überqueren*
crossroads ['krɒsrəʊdz] *Kreuzung*
crowd [kraʊd] *Menschenmenge*
crown [kraʊn] *Krone*
(to) **cry** [kraɪ] *schreien, weinen*
cucumber ['kju:kʌmbə] *Gurke*
curry ['kʌri] *Curry*
customer ['kʌstəmə] *Kunde/Kundin*

D, d

daily ['deɪli] *täglich*
(to) **dance** [dɑ:ns] *tanzen*
darling ['dɑ:lɪŋ] *Liebling, Schatz*
daughter ['dɔ:tə] *Tochter*
day [deɪ] *Tag*
(to) **daydream** ['deɪdri:m] *mit offenen Augen herumträumen*
daydreamer ['deɪdri:mə] *Tagträumer*
de facto [ˌdeɪ 'fæktəʊ] *(eheähnliche) Lebensgemeinschaft*
death [deθ] *Tod*
death penalty ['deθ penlti] *Todesstrafe*
(to) **decide** [dɪ'saɪd] *beschließen, (sich) entscheiden*
definitely ['defɪnətli] *bestimmt, sicher(lich), auf jeden Fall*
delicious [dɪ'lɪʃəs] *köstlich, lecker*
(to) **deliver** [dɪ'lɪvə] *zustellen, liefern*
dentist ['dentɪst] *Zahnarzt, Zahnärztin*
department [dɪ'pɑ:tmənt] *Abteilung*
department store [dɪ'pɑ:tmənt stɔ:] *Kauf-, Warenhaus*
desert ['dezət] *Wüste*
(to) **design** [dɪ'zaɪn] *konstruieren, entwickeln, auslegen*
desk [desk] *Schalter, Pult*
dessert [dɪ'zɜ:t] *Nachspeise, Dessert*
diary ['daɪəri] *Terminkalender*
(to) **die** [daɪ] *sterben*
different ['dɪfrənt] *verschieden, unterschiedlich*

difficult ['dɪfɪkəlt] *schwer, schwierig*
dinner ['dɪnə] *Abendessen, Essen*
  dinner jacket ['dɪnə dʒækɪt] *Smokingjacke*
directly [də'rektli] *direkt*
directory [də'rektəri] *Verzeichnis*
discerning [dɪ'sɜ:nɪŋ] *anspruchsvoll*
discipline ['dɪsəplɪn] *Disziplin*
dish [dɪʃ] *Gericht, Speise*
(to) **disturb** [dɪ'stɜ:b] *stören*
divorced [dɪ'vɔ:st] *geschieden*
(to) **do** [du:] *tun, machen, schaffen*
documentary [ˌdɒkju'mentri] *Dokumentarfilm, -sendung*
dog [dɒg] *Hund*
dollar ['dɒlə] *Dollar*
door [dɔ:] *Tür*
doorstep ['dɔ:step] *Tür(schwelle)*
dot [dɒt] *Punkt*
double ['dʌbl] *doppelt, Doppel-*
  double room [ˌdʌbl 'ru:m] *Doppelzimmer*
  double-decker bus [ˌdʌbl'dekə bʌs] *Doppeldeckerbus*
down: (to) sit down [ˌsɪt 'daʊn] *sich hinsetzen*
downstairs [ˌdaʊn'steəz] *unten*
drink [drɪŋk] *(alkoholisches) Getränk, Drink*
(to) **drink** [drɪŋk] *trinken*
(to) **drive** [draɪv] *(Auto) fahren*
driver ['draɪvə] *Fahrer/in*
  driver-only operated [draɪvər 'əʊnli ɒpəreɪtɪd] *nur mit Fahrer*
drugstore ['drʌgstɔ:] *Drogerie*
dry [draɪ] *trocken*
during ['djʊərɪŋ] *während*
dynamic [daɪ'næmɪk] *dynamisch*

E, e

each [i:tʃ] *jede/r/s*
ear [ɪə] *Ohr*
earlier ['ɜ:liə] *früher*
early ['ɜ:li] *früh, frühzeitig*
(to) **earn** [ɜ:n] *verdienen*
eastern ['i:stən] *östlich, Ost-*
easy ['i:zi] *einfach, leicht*
  easy-going [ˌi:zi 'gəʊɪŋ] *gelassen, unkompliziert*
(to) **eat** [i:t] *essen*
economics [ˌi:kə'nɒmɪks] *Wirtschaftswissenschaften*
else: anything else [ˌenɪθɪŋ 'els] *(sonst) noch etwas*
  something else [sʌmθɪŋ 'els] *noch etwas*
  where else [weər 'els] *wo sonst*
email ['i:meɪl] *E-Mail*
en suite [ˌɒ̃ 'swi:t] *mit Bad*
end [end] *Ende, Schluss*
  in the end [ɪn ði 'end] *zum Schluss, schließlich*
(to) **end** [end] *enden, aufhören*
endurance [ɪn'djʊərəns] *Ausdauer*
engaged [ɪn'geɪdʒd] *verlobt*
(to) **enjoy** [ɪn'dʒɔɪ] *genießen, gefallen, gern haben/tun*
enormous [ɪ'nɔ:məs] *enorm, gewaltig*
enough [ɪ'nʌf] *genug*
(to) **enter** ['entə] *eintreten (in)*
entrance ['entrəns] *Eingang*
equipment [ɪ'kwɪpmənt] *Ausrüstung, Ausstattung*
evening ['i:vnɪŋ] *Abend*
event [ɪ'vent] *Veranstaltung*
every ['evri] *jede/r/s*
  everyone ['evriwʌn] *jede/r/s*
  everything ['evriθɪŋ] *alles*
exact [ɪg'zækt] *genau*
excellent ['eksələnt] *ausgezeichnet, hervorragend*
except [ɪk'sept] *außer*
(to) **excuse** [ɪk'skju:z] *entschuldigen*
  Excuse me [ɪk'skju:z mi:] *Entschuldigung*
exercise ['eksəsaɪz] *Übung*
exotic [ɪg'zɒtɪk] *exotisch*
expensive [ɪk'spensɪv] *teuer*
expert ['ekspɜ:t] *Fachmann/frau, Experte/Expertin*
eye [aɪ] *Auge*

F, f

factory ['fæktəri] *Fabrik*
false [fɔ:ls] *falsch*
family ['fæməli] *Familie*
famous ['feɪməs] *berühmt*
fan [fæn] *Anhänger/in, Fan*
fantastic [fæn'tæstɪk] *fantastisch*
far [fɑ:] *weit (entfernt)*
  so far [ˌsəʊ 'fɑ:] *bislang*
fashion ['fæʃn] *Mode*
  fashion designer ['fæʃn dɪzaɪnə] *Modedesigner/in, -schöpfer/in*
fast [fɑ:st] *schnell*
  fast food [ˌfɑ:st 'fu:d] *Schnellgerichte*
father ['fɑ:ðə] *Vater*
favourite ['feɪvərɪt] *Lieblings-*
feature film ['fi:tʃə fɪlm] *Spielfilm*
fee [fi:] *Gebühr, Honorar*
(to) **feed** [fi:d] *füttern*
(to) **feel** [fi:l] *fühlen, empfinden*
feeling ['fi:lɪŋ] *Gefühl*
female ['fi:meɪl] *weiblich, Frauen-*
ferry ['feri] *Fähre*
festival ['festɪvl] *Festival, Fest(spiele)*
few: a few [ə 'fju:] *ein paar, wenige*
(to) **fight** [faɪt] *kämpfen (gegen), bekämpfen*
film [fɪlm] *Film*
  film star ['fɪlm stɑ:] *Filmstar*
(to) **find** [faɪnd] *finden*
  (to) **find out** [ˌfaɪnd 'aʊt] *herausfinden*
fine [faɪn] *gut, schön, fein*
  I'm fine [aɪm 'faɪn] *Mir geht es gut*
finger ['fɪŋgə] *Finger*
(to) **finish** ['fɪnɪʃ] *beenden, aufhören (mit), fertig werden*
fire ['faɪə] *(Kamin-)Feuer*
first [fɜ:st] *erste/r/s, zuerst*
  first aid [ˌfɜ:st 'eɪd] *erste Hilfe*
  first name ['fɜ:st neɪm] *Vorname*
  first-class [ˌfɜ:st 'klɑ:s] *erstklassig*
fish [fɪʃ] *Fisch*
fitness ['fɪtnəs] *Fitness, Kondition*
flat [flæt] *Wohnung*
flight [flaɪt] *Flug*
  flight attendant [ˌflaɪt ə'tendənt] *Flugbegleiter/in, Steward/ess*
floor plan ['flɔ: plæn] *Grundriss, Lageplan*
(to) **fly** [flaɪ] *fliegen*
(to) **follow** ['fɒləʊ] *folgen*
food [fu:d] *Essen, Lebensmittel*
football ['fʊtbɔ:l] *Fußball*
  football match ['fʊtbɔ:l mætʃ] *Fußballspiel*
for [fə] *für*
form [fɔ:m] *Form, Art*
Formula 1 [ˌfɔ:mjələ 'wʌn] *Formel 1*
free [fri:] *frei*
freedom ['fri:dəm] *Freiheit*
friend [frend] *Freund/in*
friendship ['frendʃɪp] *Freundschaft*
from [frəm] *von, aus*

front: in front of [ɪn 'frʌnt əv] *vor*
fruit [fru:t] *Obst, Frucht, Früchte*
full [fʊl] *voll, vollständig*
full-time [ˌfʊl 'taɪm] *Vollzeit-*
fully ['fʊli] *völlig, vollständig*
funny ['fʌni] *komisch, lustig*

G, g

Gaelic ['geɪlɪk] *Gälisch*
game [geɪm] *Spiel*
games machine ['geɪmz məʃi:n] *Spielautomat*
garden ['gɑ:dn] *Garten*
gardening ['gɑ:dnɪŋ] *Gartenarbeit, Gärtnern*
gay [geɪ] *schwul, lesbisch, homosexuell*
generation [ˌdʒenə'reɪʃn] *Generation*
(to) **get** [get] *bekommen, gelangen, hinkommen*
(to) **get on / off** [ˌget 'ɒn / 'ɒf] *ein-/aussteigen*
(to) **get up** [ˌget 'ʌp] *aufstehen*
girl [gɜ:l] *Mädchen*
(to) **give** [gɪv] *geben*
glass [glɑ:s] *Glas*
(to) **go** [gəʊ] *gehen, fahren*
(to) **go out** [ˌgəʊ 'aʊt] *ausgehen*
golf [gɒlf] *Golf*
gong [gɒŋ] *Gong*
good [gʊd] *gut*
government ['gʌvənmənt] *Regierung*
governor ['gʌvənə] *Gouverneur/in*
grandfather ['grænfɑ:ðə] *Großvater*
grandmother ['grænmʌðə] *Großmutter, Oma*
great [greɪt] *groß(artig), toll, prima, gut*
group [gru:p] *Gruppe, Konzern*
(to) **grow up** [ˌgrəʊ 'ʌp] *aufwachsen, erwachsen werden*
guide [gaɪd] *Führer, Handbuch*
gym [dʒɪm] *Fitnessstudio*

H, h

hairdryer ['heə draɪə] *Fön*
half [hɑ:f] *Hälfte, halb*
Halloween [ˌhæləʊ'i:n] *Halloween*
happy ['hæpi] *glücklich, fröhlich, zufrieden, froh*
happy ending [ˌhæpi 'endɪŋ] *Happy End*
harbour ['hɑ:bə] *Hafen*
hard [hɑ:d] *schwer, schwierig, hart*
hat [hæt] *Hut, Mütze*
(to) **hate** [heɪt] *hassen, überhaupt nicht mögen*
(to) **have** [hæv] *haben; essen, trinken*
(to) **have sth in common** [hæv ɪn 'kɒmən] *etw gemeinsam haben*
he [hi:] *er*
headache ['hedeɪk] *Kopfschmerzen, Kopfweh*
(to) **hear** [hɪə] *hören*
heart [hɑ:t] *Herz*
helicopter ['helɪkɒptə] *Hubschrauber*
hello [hə'ləʊ] *hallo*
help [help] *Hilfe*
(to) **help** [help] *helfen*
her [hɜ:] *ihr*
here [hɪə] *hier*
high [haɪ] *hoch*
(to) **highlight** ['haɪlaɪt] *hervorheben, markieren*
hiking ['haɪkɪŋ] *Wandern*
hill [hɪl] *Hügel, Berg*
him [hɪm] *ihn, ihm*
his [hɪz] *seine(r/s)*
history ['hɪstri] *Geschichte*

holiday ['hɒlədeɪ] *Ferien, Urlaub, Feiertag, freier Tag*
holiday flat ['hɒlədeɪ flæt] *Ferienwohnung*
holy ['həʊli] *heilig*
home [həʊm] *nach Hause, zu Hause, Zuhause*
at home [ət 'həʊm] *zu Hause*
(to) **hop on / off** [ˌhɒp 'ɒn / 'ɒf] *auf-/abspringen*
(to) **hope** [həʊp] *hoffen*
horse [hɔ:s] *Pferd*
hospital ['hɒspɪtl] *Krankenhaus*
hot [hɒt] *heiß*
hot-air balloon [ˌhɒt 'eə bəlu:n] *Heißluftballon*
hotel [həʊ'tel] *Hotel*
hour ['aʊə] *Stunde*
house [haʊs] *Haus*
househusband ['haʊshʌzbənd] *Hausmann*
housewife ['haʊswaɪf] *Hausfrau*
how [haʊ] *wie*
humour ['hju:mə] *Humor*
husband ['hʌzbənd] *(Ehe-)Mann*
hyphen ['haɪfn] *Bindestrich, Trennstrich*

I, i

idea [aɪ'dɪə] *Idee, Gedanke, Einfall*
if [ɪf] *wenn, falls, ob*
important [ɪm'pɔ:tnt] *wichtig*
in [ɪn] *in, auf*
in the end [ɪn ði 'end] *zum Schluss, schließlich*
(to) **include** [ɪn'klu:d] *enthalten, umfassen*
including [ɪn'klu:dɪŋ] *darunter, unter anderem*
information [ˌɪnfə'meɪʃn] *Auskunft, Information(en)*
information desk [ɪnfə'meɪʃn desk] *Informationsschalter, Auskunft*
(to) **inherit** [ɪn'herɪt] *erben*
inspector [ɪn'spektə] *Polizeiinspektor/in, Kommissar/in*
interested in sth ['ɪntrəstɪd ɪn] *an etw interessiert*
interesting ['ɪntrəstɪŋ] *interessant*
interests ['ɪntrəsts] *Interessen*
internet ['ɪntənet] *Internet*
internet café ['ɪntənet ˌkæfeɪ] *Internet-Café*
interview ['ɪntəvju:] *Interview*
interviewer ['ɪntəvju:ə] *Interviewer/in*
into ['ɪntə] *in … hinein*
(to) **introduce** [ˌɪntrə'dju:s] *einführen*
invitation [ˌɪnvɪ'teɪʃn] *Einladung*
(to) **invite** [ɪn'vaɪt] *einladen*
involved in sth [ɪn'vɒlvd ɪn] *beteiligt sein an, verwickelt sein in*
island ['aɪlənd] *Insel*
it [ɪt] *es*
item ['aɪtəm] *Artikel, Gegenstand*
its [ɪts] *sein/e*

J, j

jacket potato [dʒækɪt pə'teɪtəʊ] *gebackene Kartoffel*
jewellery ['dʒu:əlri] *Schmuck, Schmuckstücke*
job [dʒɒb] *Arbeit, Beruf*
jogging ['dʒɒgɪŋ] *Jogging*
journalist ['dʒɜ:nəlɪst] *Journalist/in*
journey ['dʒɜ:ni] *Reise, Fahrt*
just [dʒʌst] *nur, gerade*

K, k

(to) **keep** [ki:p] *behalten, einhalten*
kilometre ['kɪləmi:tə] *Kilometer*
kilometre per hour [ˌkɪləmi:tə pər 'aʊə] *Stundenkilometer*
kind [kaɪnd] *nett, liebenswürdig*

kitchen ['kɪtʃɪn] *Küche*
(to) **know** [nəʊ] *kennen, wissen*

L, l

lady ['leɪdi] *Dame*
lager ['lɑ:gə] *helles Bier, Lagerbier*
lake [leɪk] *See*
landmark ['lændmɑ:k] *Wahrzeichen*
landscape ['lændskeɪp] *Landschaft*
lane [leɪn] *Gasse, Weg, Spur*
language ['læŋgwɪdʒ] *Sprache*
large [lɑ:dʒ] *groß*
last [lɑ:st] *letzte/r/s, zuletzt*
late [leɪt] *spät*
(to) **laugh** [lɑ:f] *lachen*
lazy ['leɪzi] *faul, träge*
(to) **learn** [lɜ:n] *lernen, erfahren*
(to) **leave** [li:v] *abfahren, -fliegen, abreisen, weggehen, verlassen, übrig lassen*
left [left] *links*
on the left [ɒn ðə 'left] *links, auf der linken Seite*
leisure activity ['leʒə ækˈtɪvəti] *Freizeitbeschäftigung*
(to) **let** [let] *erlauben, (zu)lassen*
let's [lets] *lass/t uns, lassen Sie uns*
letter ['letə] *Buchstabe*
library ['laɪbrəri] *Bücherei, Bibliothek*
(to) **lie** [laɪ] *liegen*
life [laɪf] *Leben*
lift [lɪft] *Aufzug, Fahrstuhl*
like [laɪk] *(ähnlich) wie*
(to) **like** [laɪk] *mögen, gern haben*
lion ['laɪən] *Löwe*
(to) **listen** ['lɪsn] *zuhören*
little ['lɪtl] *klein, wenig*
(to) **live** [lɪv] *wohnen, leben*
local ['ləʊkl] *örtlich, lokal, hiesig, einheimisch*
location [ləʊ'keɪʃn] *(Stand-)Ort, Lage*
lonely ['ləʊnli] *einsam*
long [lɒŋ] *lang*
long-term [ˌlɒŋ'tɜ:m] *langfristig, Langzeit-*
(to) **look** [lʊk] *schauen, gucken, (aus)sehen*
(to) **look for** ['lʊk fə] *suchen (nach)*
(to) **lose** [lu:z] *verlieren*
lot: a lot of [ə 'lɒt əv] *viel, viele*
lots of ['lɒts əv] *viel, viele*
lottery ['lɒtəri] *Lotterie, Lotto*
loud [laʊd] *laut*
love [lʌv] *Liebe*
(to) **love** [lʌv] *lieben, sehr gern mögen*
lovely ['lʌvli] *schön, hübsch, reizend*
low [ləʊ] *niedrig*
luggage ['lʌgɪdʒ] *Gepäck*
lunch [lʌntʃ] *Mittagessen*
luxury ['lʌkʃəri] *Luxus, Luxus-*

M, m

machine: answering machine ['ɑ:nsərɪŋ məʃi:n] *Anrufbeantworter*
games machine ['geɪmz məʃi:n] *Spielautomat*
madam ['mædəm] *gnädige Frau*
magazine [ˌmægə'zi:n] *Zeitschrift, Magazin*
main [meɪn] *Haupt-*
main course [ˌmeɪn 'kɔ:s] *Hauptgericht*
(to) **make** [meɪk] *machen, zubereiten*
male [meɪl] *männlich, Männer-*
man, men [mæn, men] *Mann*
manager ['mænɪdʒə] *Manager/in*
many ['meni] *viele*
map [mæp] *Plan, Karte*
marathon ['mærəθən] *Marathon(lauf)*
marital status [ˌmærɪtl 'steɪtəs] *Familienstand*
market ['mɑ:kɪt] *(Absatz-)Markt*
marriage ['mærɪdʒ] *Ehe, Hochzeit, Eheschließung*
married ['mærid] *verheiratet*
match [mætʃ] *Spiel, Match*
may [meɪ] *dürfen, können, mögen, kann (vielleicht)*
maybe ['meɪbi] *vielleicht*
mayor [meə] *Bürgermeister/in*
me [mi:] *mir, mich*
meal [mi:l] *Essen, Mahlzeit*
(to) **mean** [mi:n] *bedeuten, heißen*
(to) **meet** [mi:t] *(sich) treffen (mit), kennen lernen*
member ['membə] *Mitglied*
menu ['menju:] *Speisekarte, Menü*
message ['mesɪdʒ] *Mitteilung, Nachricht*
midday [ˌmɪd'deɪ] *Mittag, mittags*
middle: in the middle of [ɪn ðə 'mɪdl əv] *mitten in/auf/am*
midnight ['mɪdnaɪt] *Mitternacht*
might [maɪt] *könnte(n) (vielleicht)*
mile [maɪl] *Meile*
milliner ['mɪlɪnə] *Hutmacherin*
million ['mɪljən] *Million*
millionaire [ˌmɪljə'neə] *Millionär/in*
millipede ['mɪlɪpi:d] *Tausendfüßler*
mind [maɪnd] *Gedanken*
mineral water ['mɪnərəl wɔ:tə] *Mineralwasser*
minus ['maɪnəs] *minus*
minute ['mɪnɪt] *Minute*
mobile (phone) [ˌməʊbaɪl 'fəʊn] *Mobiltelefon, Handy*
model ['mɒdl] *Modell, Model*
modern ['mɒdn] *modern*
moment ['məʊmənt] *Moment, Augenblick*
money ['mʌni] *Geld*
more [mɔ:] *mehr*
morning ['mɔ:nɪŋ] *Morgen, Vormittag*
most [məʊst] *die meisten*
mother ['mʌðə] *Mutter*
motorbike ['məʊtəbaɪk] *Motorrad*
motorway ['məʊtəweɪ] *Autobahn*
motto ['mɒtəʊ] *Motto*
mountain ['maʊntən] *(größerer) Berg*
mousse [mu:s] *Mousse*
(to) **move** [mu:v] *(sich) bewegen, umziehen*
movie ['mu:vi] *(Spiel-)Film*
moving ['mu:vɪŋ] *beweglich*
Mr ['mɪstə] *Herr*
Mrs ['mɪsɪz] *Frau*
Ms [mɪz] *Frau/Fräulein*
much [mʌtʃ] *viel*
museum [mju'zi:əm] *Museum*
music ['mju:zɪk] *Musik*
musical ['mju:zɪkl] *musikalisch*
must [mʌst] *müssen*
my [maɪ] *mein/e*

N, n

name [neɪm] *Name*
nap [næp] *Schläfchen, Nickerchen*
near [nɪə] *nahe, in der Nähe von*
nearby [ˌnɪə'baɪ] *nahe gelegen, in der Nähe*
nearly ['nɪəli] *fast*
(to) **need** [ni:d] *brauchen, benötigen*
neighbour ['neɪbə] *Nachbar/in*

neither ['naɪðə] *auch nicht, keine/r/s*
Neolithic [,ni:ə'lɪθɪk] *jungsteinzeitlich*
nervous ['nɜːvəs] *nervös*
network ['netwɜːk] *Netz(werk)*
never ['nevə] *nie(mals)*
new [njuː] *neu*
newcomer ['njuːkʌmə] *Neuling*
newspaper ['njuːzpeɪpə] *Zeitung*
next [nekst] *nächste/r/s*
  next to ['nekst tə] *(direkt) neben*
nice [naɪs] *schön, nett, hübsch*
nickname ['nɪkneɪm] *Spitzname*
niece [niːs] *Nichte*
night [naɪt] *Nacht*
no [nəʊ] *nein, kein/e*
nobody ['nəʊbədi] *niemand*
noise [nɔɪz] *Geräusch, Lärm*
non-smoker [,nɒn 'sməʊkə] *Nichtraucher/in*
normally ['nɔːməli] *normalerweise*
northwest [,nɔːθ'west] *Nordwest(en)*
nose [nəʊz] *Nase*
not [nɒt] *nicht*
notes [nəʊts] *Notizen, Aufzeichnungen*
now [naʊ] *nun, jetzt*
number ['nʌmbə] *(Telefon-)Nummer, Zahl*

O, o

o'clock [ə'klɒk] *volle Stunde, um … Uhr*
oak [əʊk] *Eiche*
odd: odd one out [ɒd wʌn 'aʊt] *das nicht dazugehörige Wort*
of [əv] *von*
  of course [əf 'kɔːs] *natürlich, selbstverständlich*
(to) **offer** ['ɒfə] *(an)bieten*
office ['ɒfɪs] *Büro*
often ['ɒfn] *oft, häufig*
old [əʊld] *alt*
on [ɒn] *auf, an, am*
once [wʌns] *sobald, wenn erst einmal*
one [wʌn] *eins, man, ein/e*
online ['ɒnlaɪn] *Online-, im/übers Internet*
only ['əʊnli] *nur, einzig*
open ['əʊpən] *offen, geöffnet*
(to) **open** ['əʊpən] *öffnen, sich öffnen*
opera ['ɒprə] *Oper*
opposite ['ɒpəzɪt] *gegenüber (liegend)*
option ['ɒpʃn] *Möglichkeit*
or [ɔː] *oder*
orchard ['ɔːtʃəd] *Obstgarten*
orchestra ['ɔːkɪstrə] *Orchester*
(to) **order** ['ɔːdə] *bestellen, in Auftrag geben*
organizer ['ɔːgənaɪzə] *Veranstalter/in*
(to) **organize** ['ɔːgənaɪz] *organisieren, arrangieren*
other ['ʌðə] *andere/r/s*
our ['aʊə] *unser/e*
out [aʊt] *aus, draußen, hinaus/heraus*
outdoor ['aʊtdɔː] *im Freien*
outstanding [aʊt'stændɪŋ] *hervorragend*
over ['əʊvə] *über*
  over there [,əʊvə 'ðeə] *da drüben*
overground ['əʊvəgraʊnd] *oberirdisch*
overlooking [,əʊvə'lʊkɪŋ] *mit Blick hinunter auf*
own [əʊn] *eigene/r/s*
owner ['əʊnə] *Besitzer/in, Eigentümer/in*

P, p

p.m. [,piː 'em] *von Mittag bis Mitternacht*
(to) **pack** [pæk] *packen*
page [peɪdʒ] *Seite*
(to) **paint** [peɪnt] *malen*
parents ['peərənts] *Eltern*
park [pɑːk] *Park*
part [pɑːt] *Teil*
  part-time [,pɑːt'taɪm] *Teilzeit-, Teilzeit*
partner ['pɑːtnə] *Partner/in, Gesellschafter/in*
party ['pɑːti] *Party, Fest, Feier*
passenger ['pæsɪndʒə] *Passagier/in, Fahr-, Fluggast*
passport ['pɑːspɔːt] *Reisepass, Pass*
past [pɑːst] *nach*
  (to) **go past sth** [,gəʊ 'pɑːst] *an etw vorbeigehen*
(to) **pause** [pɔːz] *innehalten, anhalten*
(to) **pay** [peɪ] *(be)zahlen*
  pay point ['peɪ pɔɪnt] *Zahlstelle*
peak hours ['piːk aʊəz] *Rushhour, Stoßzeit*
people ['piːpl] *Leute, Menschen*
perhaps [pə'hæps] *vielleicht, eventuell*
person ['pɜːsn] *Mensch, Person*
personal ['pɜːsənl] *persönlich, privat*
personally ['pɜːsənəli] *persönlich*
petrol station ['petrəl steɪʃn] *Tankstelle*
phone [fəʊn] *Telefon*
  phone call ['fəʊn kɔːl] *Anruf, Telefongespräch*
  phone number ['fəʊn nʌmbə] *Telefonnummer*
(to) **phone** [fəʊn] *telefonieren, anrufen*
photo ['fəʊtəʊ] *Foto*
phrase [freɪz] *(Rede-)Wendung, Ausdruck*
physical ['fɪzɪkl] *körperlich*
piano bar [pi'ænəʊ bɑː] *Piano-Bar*
(to) **pick up** [,pɪk 'ʌp] *aufheben, hochheben*
picture ['pɪktʃə] *Bild*
pilot ['paɪlət] *Pilot/in*
pint [paɪnt] *Pint*
pizza ['piːtsə] *Pizza*
place [pleɪs] *Stelle, Platz, Ort*
  place of birth [,pleɪs əv 'bɜːθ] *Geburtsort*
(to) **plan** [plæn] *planen, vorhaben*
plane [pleɪn] *Flugzeug*
plaster ['plɑːstə] *Pflaster*
platform ['plætfɔːm] *Plattform*
play: play on words [,pleɪ ɒn 'wɜːdz] *Wortspiel*
(to) **play** [pleɪ] *spielen*
player ['pleɪə] *Spieler/in*
playground ['pleɪgraʊnd] *Spielplatz*
pleasant ['pleznt] *angenehm*
please [pliːz] bitte
ploughman's lunch [,plaʊmənz 'lʌntʃ] *Imbiss aus Brot, Käse und Pickles*
plus [plʌs] *plus*
political [pə'lɪtɪkl] *politisch*
politician [,pɒlə'tɪʃn] *Politiker/in*
poor [pʊə] *arm, schlecht, mangelhaft*
pop group ['pɒp gruːp] *Popgruppe*
pop music ['pɒp mjuːzɪk] *Popmusik*
popular ['pɒpjələ] *beliebt, populär*
population [,pɒpju'leɪʃn] *Bevölkerung*
postcard ['pəʊstkɑːd] *Postkarte*
potato [pə'teɪtəʊ] *Kartoffel*
  potato crisps [pə'teɪtəʊ krɪsps] *Kartoffelchips*
pound [paʊnd] *Pfund*
power steering ['paʊə stɪərɪŋ] *Servolenkung*
(to) **prefer** [prɪ'fɜː] *vorziehen, lieber mögen, bevorzugen*
(to) **prepare** [prɪ'peə] *(sich) vorbereiten, zubereiten*

present ['preznt] *Geschenk; Gegenwart, Präsens*
president ['prezɪdənt] *Präsident/in*
(to) **press** [pres] *drücken*
press review ['pres rɪvju:] *Presseüberblick*
price [praɪs] *(Kauf-)Preis*
prize [praɪz] *Preis, Gewinn*
problem ['prɒbləm] *Problem*
professional [prə'feʃənl] *professionell*
programme ['prəʊgræm] *Sendung, Programm*
programmer ['prəʊgræmə] *Programmierer/in*
(to) **promote** [prə'məʊt] *unterstützen, promoten, Werbung machen für*
(to) **provide** [prə'vaɪd] *zur Verfügung stellen, anbieten*
pub [pʌb] *Kneipe, Pub*
public transport [ˌpʌblɪk 'trænspɔ:t] *öffentliche Verkehrsmittel*
(to) **pull** [pʊl] *ziehen, zerren*
(to) **push** [pʊʃ] *schieben, stoßen*
(to) **put** [pʊt] setzen, *stellen, legen*
(to) **put to bed** [ˌpʊt tə 'bed] *ins Bett bringen*

Q, q

quarter ['kwɔ:tə] *(ein) Viertel*
quarter past ['kwɔ:tə pɑ:st] *Viertel nach*
quarter to ['kwɔ:tə tə] *Viertel vor*
question ['kwestʃən] *Frage*
quickly ['kwɪkli] *schnell, rasch*
quiet ['kwaɪət] *still, ruhig, leise*
quite [kwaɪt] *ziemlich, ganz*
quiz show ['kwɪz ʃəʊ] *Quizshow, Ratesendung*

R, r

rain [reɪn] *Regen*
(to) **rain** [reɪn] *regnen*
rainy ['reɪni] *regnerisch*
range [reɪndʒ] *Auswahl, Palette*
(to) **read** [ri:d] *lesen*
ready ['redi] *fertig, bereit*
real [rɪəl] *echt, wirklich*
really ['ri:əli] *wirklich, eigentlich, tatsächlich*
(to) **receive** [rɪ'si:v] *erhalten*
recent ['ri:snt] *jünger*
(to) **recognise** ['rekəgnaɪz] *erkennen*
recreational activities [ˌrekri'eɪʃənl ækˌtɪvɪti:s] *Freizeitaktivitäten*
red [red] *rot*
(to) **reduce** [rɪ'dju:s] *reduzieren*
regular ['regjələ] *regelmäßig, planmäßig*
relationship [rɪ'leɪʃnʃɪp] *Beziehung*
relatives ['relətɪvz] *Verwandte*
(to) **relax** [rɪ'læks] *(sich) entspannen, sich ausruhen*
relaxed [rɪ'lækst] *entspannt*
(to) **remember** [rɪ'membə] *sich (an etw) erinnern*
(to) **repeat** [rɪ'pi:t] *wiederholen*
Republican [rɪ'pʌblɪkən] *Republikaner/in, republikanisch*
residential area [rezɪˌdenʃl 'eəriə] *Wohngebiet*
rest [rest] *Rest*
restaurant ['restrɒnt] *Restaurant*
(to) **retire** [rɪ'taɪə] *sich zur Ruhe setzen, in Rente/Pension gehen*
review [rɪ'vju:] *Rezension, Kritik*
rice [raɪs] *Reis*
right [raɪt] *rechts, richtig, genau*
on the right [ɒn ðə 'raɪt] *rechts, auf der rechten Seite*
river ['rɪvə] *Fluss*
road [rəʊd] *(Land-)Straße*
roll [rəʊl] *Brötchen*
room [ru:m] *Zimmer, Raum*
round [raʊnd] *um (... herum)*
routine [ru:'ti:n] *Routine(arbeit), Tagesablauf*
(to) **run** [rʌn] *laufen*
rural ['rʊərəl] *ländlich*

S, s

salad ['sæləd] *Salat*
sales [seɪlz] *Vertrieb, Verkauf*
salmon ['sæmən] *Lachs*
(the) **same** [seɪm] *der/die/das gleiche, der-, die-, dasselbe*
at the same time [ət ðə ˌseɪm 'taɪm] *gleichzeitig*
sandals ['sændlz] *Sandalen*
sandwich ['sænwɪdʒ] *Sandwich*
sauna ['sɔ:nə] *Sauna*
(to) **say** [seɪ] *sagen*
schedule ['ʃedju:l] *Zeitplan*
school [sku:l] *Schule*
seat [si:t] *Sitz(platz)*
second ['sekənd] *zweite(r,s)*
secondhand [ˌsekənd'hænd] *gebraucht, aus zweiter Hand*
secretary ['sekrətri] *Sekretär/in*
(to) **see** [si:] *sehen, verstehen, treffen*
(to) **seem** [si:m] *(er)scheinen*
seldom ['seldəm] *selten*
selection [sɪ'lekʃn] *Auswahl, Angebot*
(to) **sell** [sel] *verkaufen*
(to) **send** [send] *senden, schicken*
sense [sens] *Sinn*
separated ['sepəreɪtɪd] *getrennt*
serious ['sɪəriəs] *ernst, ernsthaft*
(to) **serve** [sɜ:v] *servieren, bedienen, anbieten*
service ['sɜ:vɪs] *Betrieb*
session ['seʃn] *Treffen, Session*
sex [seks] *Geschlecht*
shadow ['ʃædəʊ] *Schatten*
she [ʃi:] *sie*
shellfish ['ʃelfɪʃ] *Schalentier*
ship [ʃɪp] *Schiff*
shoe [ʃu:] *Schuh*
shop [ʃɒp] *Laden, Geschäft*
shopping ['ʃɒpɪŋ] *Einkauf(en)*
shoreline ['ʃɔ:laɪn] *Uferlinie*
short [ʃɔ:t] *kurz*
should [ʃʊd] *solle/n, sollte/n*
show [ʃəʊ] *Unterhaltungssendung, Show*
(to) **show** [ʃəʊ] *zeigen, vorzeigen*
(to) **show sb around** [ˌʃəʊ ə'raʊnd] *jdn herumführen*
shower ['ʃaʊə] *Dusche*
shy [ʃaɪ] *schüchtern, scheu*
side [saɪd] *Seite*
side by side [ˌsaɪd baɪ 'saɪd] *nebeneinander, Seite an Seite*
sights [saɪts] *Sehenswürdigkeiten*
sightseeing tour ['saɪtsi:ɪŋ tʊə] *Stadtrundfahrt*
simple ['sɪmpl] *einfach*
simply ['sɪmpli] *einfach*
since [sɪns] *seit*
(to) **sing** [sɪŋ] *singen*
singer ['sɪŋə] *Sänger/in*
single ['sɪŋgl] *alleinstehend*
single room [ˌsɪŋgl 'ru:m] *Einzelzimmer*
sir [sɜ:] *mein Herr*
sister ['sɪstə] *Schwester*
(to) **sit** [sɪt] *sitzen, sich hinsetzen*
(to) **sit down** [ˌsɪt 'daʊn] *sich (hin)setzen*
skiing ['ski:ɪŋ] *Skilaufen*
slash [slæʃ] *Schrägstrich*
(to) **sleep** [sli:p] *schlafen*

slow [sləʊ] *langsam*
small [smɔ:l] *klein*
smart [smɑ:t] *schick, flott*
(to) **smell** [smel] *riechen*
smoke free ['sməʊk fri:] *rauchfrei*
smoked [sməʊkt] *geräuchert*
snack [snæk] *Imbiss*
so [səʊ] *so, so dass, also*
software ['sɒftweə] *Software, Computerprogramm(e)*
some [sʌm] *einige, etwas*
  someone ['sʌmwʌn] *jemand*
  something ['sʌmθɪŋ] *etwas*
  sometimes ['sʌmtaɪmz] *manchmal*
son [sʌn] *Sohn*
song [sɒŋ] *Lied*
sorry ['sɒri] *tut mir Leid, Entschuldigung*
sort [sɔ:t] *Art, Sorte, Typ*
soup [su:p] *Suppe*
southern ['sʌðən] *Süd-, südlich*
souvenir [ˌsu:və'nɪə] *Andenken, Souvenir*
spacious ['speɪʃəs] *weitläufig, geräumig*
spaghetti [spə'geti] *Spaghetti*
(to) **speak** [spi:k] *sprechen, reden*
specialty ['speʃəlti] *Spezialität*
(to) **spell** [spel] *buchstabieren, schreiben*
(to) **spend** [spend] *(Geld) ausgeben, (Zeit) verbringen*
spirits ['spɪrɪts] *Spirituosen*
sport [spɔ:t] *Sport, Sportart*
sports [spɔ:ts] *Sport*
(to) **spot** [spɒt] *erkennen*
square kilometre ['skweə kɪləmi:tə] *Quadratkilometer*
square mile ['skweə maɪl] *Quadratmeile*
stairs [steəz] *Treppe(n)*
stamp [stæmp] *Briefmarke*
standard ['stændəd] *Standard, Standard-*
star [stɑ:] *Star*
(to) **start** [stɑ:t] *beginnen, starten*
state [steɪt] *(Bundes-)Staat*
station ['steɪʃn] *Bahnhof*
(to) **stay** [steɪ] *bleiben, übernachten*
steering ['stɪərɪŋ] *Lenkung*
still [stɪl] *(immer) noch, noch immer*
(to) **stop** [stɒp] *einstellen, beenden*
store [stɔ:] *Laden, Geschäft*
story ['stɔ:ri] *Erzählung, Geschichte*
straight [streɪt] *direkt*
street [stri:t] *Straße*
strong [strɒŋ] *stark*
(to) **struggle** ['strʌgl] *kämpfen*
student ['stju:dnt] *Student/in*
study ['stʌdi] *Arbeitszimmer*
successful [sək'sesfl] *erfolgreich*
such (a) [sʌtʃ] *so(lch) ein*
suitcase ['su:tkeɪs] *Koffer*
sun [sʌn] *Sonne*
sunglasses ['sʌnglɑ:sɪz] *Sonnenbrille*
sunny ['sʌni] *sonnig*
sunscreen ['sʌnskri:n] *Sonnenmilch, -creme*
super star ['su:pə stɑ:] *Superstar*
superb [su:'pɜ:b] *hervorragend*
superior [su:'pɪəriə] *gehoben*
(to) **support** [sə'pɔ:t] *unterstützen, befürworten*
sure [ʃʊə] *sicher*
(to) **surf** [sɜ:f] *surfen*
surname ['sɜ:neɪm] *Nach-, Familienname*
surrounding [sə'raʊndɪŋ] *umgebend, umliegend*
swan [swɒn] *Schwan*
(to) **swim** [swɪm] *schwimmen*
(to) **switch off / on** [ˌswɪtʃ 'ɒf / 'ɒn] *aus-, / einschalten*
system administrator [ˌsɪstəm əd'mɪnɪstreɪtə] *Systemverwalter/in*

T, t

table ['teɪbl] *Tisch*
(to) **take** [teɪk] *nehmen, dauern*
  (to) **take a nap** [ˌteɪk ə 'næp] *ein Nickerchen machen*
  (to) **take it easy** [ˌteɪk ɪt 'i:zi] *sich schonen*
  (to) **take notes** [teɪk 'nəʊts] *(sich) Notizen machen*
talent ['tælənt] *Talent, Begabung*
(to) **talk** [tɔ:k] *sprechen, reden*
(to) **taste** [teɪst] *schmecken*
tax [tæks] *Steuer(n)*
taxi ['tæksi] *Taxi*
tea [ti:] *Tee*
teacher ['ti:tʃə] *Lehrer/in*
team [ti:m] *Mannschaft*
technological [ˌteknə'lɒdʒɪkl] *technologisch*
telephone ['telɪfəʊn] *Telefon*
television ['telɪvɪʒn] *Fernsehen, Fernseher*
  television tower ['telɪvɪʒn taʊə] *Fernsehturm*
teleworker ['teliwɜ:kə] *Heimarbeiter/in am Computer*
(to) **tell** [tel] *sagen, erzählen, nennen*
tennis ['tenɪs] *Tennis*
than [ðən] *als*
thank you ['θæŋk ju:] *danke*
thanks [θæŋks] *danke*
that [ðæt] *dies, der, die, das, dass, jene/r/s*
the [ðə, ði] *der/die/das, die*
their [ðeə] *ihr/e*
them [ðem] *ihnen, sie (3. Person Plural)*
then [ðen] *dann*
there [ðeə] *da, dort, dorthin*
these [ði:z] *diese*
they [ðeɪ] *sie (3. Person Plural)*
thing [θɪŋ] *Sache, Ding, Gegenstand*
(to) **think** [θɪŋk] *denken, meinen, finden, glauben*
third [θɜ:d] *dritte/r/s*
third-rate ['θɜ:dreɪt] *drittklassig*
thirsty ['θɜ:sti] *durstig*
this [ðɪs] *dies, diese/r/s*
those [ðəʊz] *jene*
through [θru:] *durch … hindurch, durch*
(to) **tick** [tɪk] *ankreuzen, markieren*
ticket ['tɪkɪt] *(Fahr-)Karte, (Flug-)Ticket*
till [tɪl] *bis*
time [taɪm] *Zeit*
tired ['taɪəd] *müde*
title ['taɪtl] *Titel, Bezeichnung*
to [tə, tʊ, tu:] *zu, nach*
toast [təʊst] *Toast, Toastbrot*
today [tə'deɪ] *heute*
together [tə'geðə] *zusammen*
toilet ['tɔɪlət] *Toilette*
toll [təʊl] *Maut(gebühr)*
tomato [tə'mɑ:təʊ] *Tomate*
tomorrow [tə'mɒrəʊ] *morgen*
tongue [tʌŋ] *Zunge*
too [tu:] *zu, auch*
(to) **touch** [tʌtʃ] *berühren*
tour [tʊə] *Tour, Rundgang, -fahrt, -reise, Führung*
tourist ['tʊərɪst] *Tourist/in*
town [taʊn] *Stadt*
toy [tɔɪ] *Spielzeug*
traditional [trə'dɪʃənl] *traditionell*

traffic ['træfɪk] *(Straßen-)Verkehr*
traffic jam ['træfɪk dʒæm] *Verkehrsstau, Stau, Verkehrschaos*
traffic lights ['træfɪk laɪts] *(Verkehrs-)Ampel*
train [treɪn] *Zug*
training ['treɪnɪŋ] *Training*
transport ['trænspɔ:t] *Transport, Beförderung, Verkehrsmittel*
travel ['trævl] *Reisen, Reise-*
(to) **travel** ['trævl] *reisen, bereisen*
trinity ['trɪnəti] *Dreifaltigkeit*
trip [trɪp] *Ausflug, Reise*
true [tru:] *richtig, wahr, zutreffend*
(to) **try** [traɪ] *(aus-, an)probieren, kosten, versuchen*
tube [tju:b] *U-Bahn*
(to) **turn left/right** [tɜ:n 'left 'raɪt] *nach links/rechts abbiegen*
TV [ˌti: 'vi:] *Fernsehen, -seher*
TV presenter [ti:ˌvi: prɪ'zentə] *Fernsehmoderator/in*
twin room [ˌtwɪn 'ru:m] *Zweibettzimmer*
typical ['tɪpɪkl] *typisch, charakteristisch*

U, u

umbrella [ʌm'brelə] *(Regen-)Schirm*
uncle ['ʌŋkl] *Onkel*
under ['ʌndə] *unter*
underground ['ʌndəgraʊnd] *U-Bahn*
underscore [ˌʌndə'skɔ:] *Unterstrich*
unfortunately [ʌn'fɔ:tʃənətli] *unglücklicherweise, leider*
universe ['ju:nɪvɜ:s] *Universum*
university [ˌju:nɪ'vɜ:səti] *Universität*
until [ən'tɪl] *bis*
up [ʌp] *oben , nach oben, hinauf, herauf*
up to ['ʌp tə] *bis zu*
upstairs [ˌʌp'steəz] *die Treppe hinauf, (nach) oben, im oberen Stockwerk*
us [ʌs] *uns*
(to) **use** [ju:z] *benutzen, verwenden*
user ['ju:zə] *Anwender/in, Benutzer/in*
usually ['ju:ʒuəli] *normalerweise, gewöhnlich, meistens*

V, v

variety [və'raɪəti] *Vielfalt*
vegetable ['vedʒtəbl] *Gemüse*
vegetarian [ˌvedʒə'teəriən] *Vegetarier/in, vegetarisch*
vehicle ['vi:əkl] *Fahrzeug, (Verkehrs-)Mittel*
very ['veri] *sehr*
veteran car ['vetərən kɑ:] *Oldtimer*
video camera ['vɪdiəʊ kæmərə] *Videokamera*
video projector ['vɪdiəʊ prəˌdʒektə] *Beamer*
view [vju:] *Ansicht, Aussicht*
village ['vɪlɪdʒ] *Dorf*
violent ['vaɪələnt] *brutal*
(to) **visit** ['vɪzɪt] *besuchen, besichtigen*
visitor ['vɪzɪtə] *Besucher/in, Gast*

W, w

(to) **wait** [weɪt] *warten*
waiter ['weɪtə] *Kellner, Ober*
waitress ['weɪtrəs] *Kellnerin*
(to) **walk** [wɔ:k] *Spaziergang, (zu Fuß) gehen*
walking boots ['wɔ:kɪŋ bu:ts] *Wanderschuhe*
(to) **wander off** [ˌwɒndər 'ɒf] *umherwandern, abschweifen*
(to) **want** [wɒnt] *wollen*
warm [wɔ:m] *warm*
(to) **waste time** [weɪst 'taɪm] *Zeit verschwenden*
(to) **watch** [wɒtʃ] *zusehen, an-, zuschauen*
(to) **watch out** [ˌwɒtʃ 'aʊt] *aufpassen*
water ['wɔ:tə] *Wasser*
water-skiing ['wɔ:təski:ɪŋ] *Wasserski (laufen)*
way [weɪ] *Weg, Art und Weise*
we [wi:] *wir*
weather ['weðə] *Wetter*
week [wi:k] *Woche*
weekday ['wi:kdeɪ] *Wochentag, Werktag*
weekend [ˌwi:k'end] *Wochenende*
welcome ['welkəm] *willkommen*
west [west] *Westen*
wet [wet] *nass, feucht*
what [wɒt] *was, welche/r/s*
wheelchair ['wi:ltʃeə] *Rollstuhl*
when [wen] *wenn, als, wann*
whenever [wen'evə] *immer wenn, wann immer*
where [weə] *wo, wohin*
which [wɪtʃ] *welche/r/s*
while [waɪl] *während*
whisky ['wɪski] *Whisky*
white [waɪt] *weiß*
who [hu:] *wer, der/die/das, welche(r/s)*
why [waɪ] *warum*
wide [waɪd] *breit, weit*
widowed ['wɪdəʊd] *verwitwet*
wife [waɪf] *(Ehe-)Frau*
will [wɪl] *Wille*
window ['wɪndəʊ] *Fenster*
wine [waɪn] *Wein*
winter ['wɪntə] *Winter*
with [wɪð, wɪθ] *mit, bei*
woman, women ['wʊmən, 'wɪmɪn] *Frau, Frauen*
wonderful ['wʌndəfl] *wunderbar, wundervoll*
word [wɜ:d] *Wort*
work [wɜ:k] *Arbeit*
(to) **work** [wɜ:k] *arbeiten*
workaholic [ˌwɜ:kə'hɒlɪk] *Arbeitswütige/r, Arbeitssüchtige/r*
worker ['wɜ:kə] *Arbeiter/in*
working hours [ˌwɜ:kɪŋ 'aʊəz] *Arbeitszeit*
workplace ['wɜ:kpleɪs] *Arbeitsplatz*
world [wɜ:ld] *Welt*
(to) **worry** ['wʌri] *sich Sorgen machen*
worse [wɜ:s] *schlechter, schlimmer*
worth [wɜ:θ] *wert, lohnend*
would [wʊd] *würde/st/n*
(to) **write** [raɪt] *schreiben*
wrong [rɒŋ] *falsch*

Y, y

year [jɪə] *Jahr*
yes [jes] *ja*
yesterday ['jestədeɪ] *gestern*
you [ju:] *du, Sie, ihr, dich, dir, Ihnen, euch, man*
young [jʌŋ] *jung*
your [jɔ:] *dein/e, Ihr/e, euer/e*
yourself [jɔ:'self] *du/Sie selbst, (Sie) sich, sich selbst*

Z, z

zone [zəʊn] *Zone, Bereich*

Die **farbig** hervorgehobenen Begriffe kennzeichnen Wörter und Wendungen aus den Bereichen „The Real Thing", die sonst nicht im Wortschatz des *Extra Language Trainer* vorkommen.

Hinweise zur Aussprache

ɑ: wie in **a**sk [ɑ:sk]
ʌ wie in b**u**s [bʌs]
æ wie in c**a**n [kæn]
e wie in **e**ntertainment [ˌentə'teɪnmənt]
i: wie in h**e** [hi:]
i wie in happ**y** ['hæpɪ]
ɪ wie in s**i**t [sɪt]
ɜ: wie in b**ir**thday [bɜ:θdeɪ]
ɒ wie in g**o**t [gɒt]
ɔ: wie in sh**or**ts [ʃɔ:ts]
ʊ wie in b**oo**k [bʊk]
u: wie in f**oo**d [fu:d]
u wie in sit**u**ation [ˌsɪtʃu'eɪʃn]
ə wie in fath**er** ['fɑ:ðə]
aɪ wie in fl**igh**t ['flaɪt]
aʊ wie in br**ow**se ['braʊz]
eɪ wie in d**a**te [deɪt]
ɔɪ wie in b**oy** [bɔɪ]
ɪə wie in h**ear** [hɪə]
eə wie in h**air** [heə]
əʊ wie in ph**o**ne [fəʊn]
ʊə wie in s**ure** [ʃʊə]
ŋ wie in darli**ng** ['dɑ:lɪŋ]
s wie in **s**orry ['sɒri]
z wie in **z**ero ['zɪərəʊ]
ʃ wie in **sh**op [ʃɒp]
tʃ wie in **ch**icken ['tʃɪkɪn]
dʒ wie in **j**ob [dʒɒb]
v wie in **v**ideo rental ['vɪdiəʊ ˌrentl]
r wie in **r**adio [ˌreɪdɪəʊ]
ʒ wie in televi**si**on ['telɪvɪʒn]
θ wie in **th**ree [θri:]
ð wie in **th**is [ðɪs]
w wie in **w**onderful ['wʌndəfʊl]

Verwendete Abkürzungen

etw	etwas
jdn	jemanden
sb	somebody
sth	something

Country	Nationality	Language
Albania	Albanian	Albanian, Greek
Algeria	Algerian	Arabic, French, Berber
Andorra	Andorran	Catalan, French, Spanish
Austria	Austrian	German, Slovene, Croatian
Belarus	Belarusian	Belarusian, Russian, Polish
Belgium	Belgian	Dutch, French, German
Bosnia and Herzegovina	Bosnian, Herzegovinian	Bosnian, Croatian, Serbian
Bulgaria	Bulgarian	Bulgarian, Turkish, Roma
Croatia	Croatian	Croatian, Serbian
Czech Republic	Czech	Czech
Denmark	Danish	Danish, Faroese
Estonia	Estonian	Estonian, Russian
Finland	Finnish	Finnish, Swedish
France	French	French
Germany	German	German
Great Britain	British	English, Welsh, (Scottish) Gaelic
Greece	Greek	Greek
Hungary	Hungarian	Hungarian
Iceland	Icelandic	Icelandic
Ireland	Irish	English, Irish Gaelic
Italy	Italian	Italian
Latvia	Latvian	Latvian, Russian, Lithuanian
Lithuania	Lithuanian	Lithuanian, Polish, Russian
Luxembourg	Luxembourg	Luxembourgish, German, French
Macedonia	Macedonian	Macedonian, Albanian, Turkish
Malta	Maltese	Maltese, English
Moldova	Moldovan	Moldovan, Russian, Gagauz
Monaco	Monacan, Monegasque	French, English, Italian, Monegasque
Morocco	Moroccan	Arabic, Berber, French
Netherlands	Dutch	Dutch, Frisian
Norway	Norwegian	Norwegian
Northern Ireland	(Northern) Irish, British	English
Poland	Polish	Polish
Portugal	Portuguese	Portuguese, Mirandese
Romania	Romanian	Romanian, Hungarian, German
Russia	Russian	Russian, Tatar, Ukranian
Scotland	Scottish, British	English, (Scottish) Gaelic
Serbia and Montenegro	Serbian; Montenegrin	Serbian; Albanian, Montenegrin
Slovakia	Slovak	Slovak, Hungarian, Roma
Slovenia	Slovenian	Slovenian, Serbo-Croatian
Spain	Spanish	Spanish, Catalan, Galician, Basque
Sweden	Swedish	Swedish, Sami, Finnish
Switzerland	Swiss	German, French, Italian,
Tunisia	Tunisian	Arabic, French
Turkey	Turkish	Turkish, Kurdish, Arabic
Ukraine	Ukranian	Ukranian, Russian
United Kingdom	British	English, Welsh, Scottish Gaelic
Wales	Welsh	English, Welsh

Eine Übersicht mit weiteren geographischen Begriffen finden Sie in den *Phrase-books* der Kursbücher.

First Choice
Englisch für Erwachsene

A1 Extra Language Trainer

Im Auftrag des Verlages erarbeitet von	John Stevens, Bad Münstereifel Marion Karg, Schwäbisch Gmünd Frauke Mönkeberg, Bielefeld: *My Portfolio*, *The Real Thing* Units 9, 11 und 12
Beratende Mitarbeit	Christine House, Berlin Frauke Mönkeberg, Bielefeld Silvia Nienhaus, Bergisch-Gladbach Dietlind Unger, Leipzig
Redaktion	Martin Maier
Redaktionelle Mitarbeit	Christine House, Oliver Busch (Wortliste), Dr. Sabine Krämer (Phonetik)
Bildredaktion	Uta Hübner
Projektleitung	Helga Holtkamp
Illustration	Christian Bartz, Berlin: S. 9, 12, 24, 30, 36, 43, 44, 47, 50 Dylan Gibson, Glasgow: S. 56, 71, 72, 73 Oxford Designers & Illustrators: S. 6, 10, 16, 24, 30, 36, 42, 50, 56
Umschlag, Layout und technische Umsetzung	Knut Waisznor
Weitere Materialien	**Extra Language Trainer** mit CD-ROM ISBN-13: 978-3-464-01940-3 / ISBN-10: 3-464-01940-5

Textquellen:
S. 22: © 2003 by Rebecca Murray (http://movies.about.com). Used with permission of About, Inc. Which can be found on the Web at www.about.com All rights reserved

Bildquellen:
Alamy: S. 42/D. Sanger Photography, S. 51/allOver photography, S. 67 KeyCollection-21 Carrot; *Bananastock*: S. 11, 17, 21, 65; *Bielefeld Marketing GmbH*: S. 49, 63; *Bilderbox*: S. 75/E. *Wodicka*; *British Airways*: S. 34; *Buckstegen*, C.: S. 16; *Chipps, J.*: S. 70; *Comstock*: S. 6, 17, 18 (2), 25; *Corbis GmbH*: S. 6/RF, S. 8/Vincent/Coopman, 20/RF, S. 25/RF, S. 26/RF, S. 32/RF, S. 33/RF, S. 34/RF/J. Craigmyle (2), S. 43/Stock4B, S. 45/T. Hemmings, S. 70/RF, S. 75/RF, S. 78/Star/P. Leonard (2), S. 79/Cameron; *Corel Library*: S. 6 (2), 8 (5), 18 (2), 23, 35, 38, 41, 42 (5), 49 (4), 52, 58, 59, 60, 63 (4), 64, 70 (5); *Das Fotoarchiv*: S. 39/J. Powell, S. 63/M. Vollmer; *defd pwe-Verlag GmbH*: S. 22 (It runs in the family), S. 62 (Terminator III); easyJet: S. 42; *Fast Impressions*: S. 68; *Getty Images*: S. 10/K. Murray, S. 20/R. Lockyer, S. 31/M. Powell, S. 38/RF (3), S. 46/S. Simpson, S. 62/AFP, S. 65/B. Laurance, S. 66/B. Ayres, S. 76/RF; *ifa-Bilderteam*: S. 57/P. Grüner; *ips, International Publishing Services für Cornelsen Verlag*: S. 10; *Jahreszeiten Verlag*: S. 27; *Karg, M.*: S. 28; *Maier, M.*: S. 8, 49, 63; *Melitta*: S. 34; *Oxford City Council*: S. 28 (2); *Picture-alliance*: S. 42/Photoshot, S. 49/ZB, S. 60/Photoshot (2),/KPA-HIP-Ann Ronan, S. 62/dpa (2), S. 63/ZB/dpa, S. 75/KPA; *Piz Buin*: S. 70; *Routemasters (www.routemasters.co.uk)*: S. 80/R. Obergfell; *Transport for London*: S. 48; *Waisznor, K.*: S. 55; *Widmann, Peter*: S. 61

Reproduktionen:
S. 10: Barclays; S. 14: Copyright Commonwealth of Australia reproduced by permission; S. 40: The Radio Times Magazine; S. 48: Transport for London; S. 54: Visit Orkney (www.visitorkney.com); S. 75: moBiel GmbH, Bielefeld

www.cornelsen.de

Die Internetadressen und -dateien, die in diesem Lehrwerk angegeben sind, wurden vor Drucklegung geprüft. Der Verlag übernimmt keine Gewähr für die Aktualität und den Inhalt dieser Adressen und Dateien oder solcher, die mit ihnen verlinkt sind.

1. Auflage, 1. Druck 2006

Alle Drucke dieser Auflage sind inhaltlich unverändert und können im Unterricht nebeneinander verwendet werden.

Druck: aprinta, Wemding

ISBN-13: 978-3-464-01942-9

ISBN-10: 3-464-01942-X

Inhalt gedruckt auf säurefreiem Papier aus nachhaltiger Forstwirtschaft.